The Secret Language of Your Face

Chi An Kuei

The Secret Language of Your Face

The Ancient Chinese Art of Siang Mien

Translated by Rosemary Dear

Souvenir Press

Contents

Introduction

Our longing to discover something about our own destiny is as old as humanity itself. So it is not surprising that the origins of the Chinese art of reading faces go back more than 3,000 years. *Siang Mien*, the art of reading faces, was already flourishing in the time of Confucius, the founder of Chinese religious education. One of the sayings of Confucius is: 'A child can do nothing about his face, but an adult is responsible for his own appearance.'

The wisdom of *Siang Mien* has always been kept secret, passed down through the generations from master to pupil.

Books about *Siang Mien*, in which the lore of fortune-telling and the interpretation of faces was set down, existed from the earliest times, but they were only accessible to the Chinese emperors and were guarded as treasure.

Just how much the ruler was influenced by the art of reading faces is shown, for example, by the Emperor Tsin-Che-Wong, who ruled the Middle Kingdom in 221 BC. This power-mad despot ordered all the literature in his kingdom to be burned—part of which consisted of the priceless writings from the time of Confucius, including the books on reading faces. He did this in the belief that these writings would expose him as an evil and treacherous tyrant. Fear of the discovery of his true character went so deep that he flatly refused to let his court painter portray him as he was, even though the custom of the time demanded it. He ordered a completely different portrait to be painted—with a face showing all the most auspicious features which would convince his subjects of his goodness and benevolence.

Much of what is known about *Siang Mien* today has been handed down orally, and this age-old wisdom was later expanded through the knowledge of *Siang Mien* masters who travelled the world to examine the faces of people in foreign countries.

Many other forms of fortune-telling which originated in China have lost their importance or are used today simply as party games. But *Siang Mien* has survived: because, right up to the present day, the face has lost nothing of its importance as the mirror of the soul.

We can learn a great deal about the people in our lives through their faces. Those who master the art of interpreting them will be able to gain a deeper knowledge than their fellows of the people they meet. But we mustn't forget the medical aspect of *Siang Mien*. In Chinese medicine treatment always includes an analysis of the face. For example, small teeth with gaps between them indicate that in his youth this patient ate predominantly animal protein, while excessively large molars and incisors point to a natural diet with a high proportion of cereals. And the eyes tell us at a glance whether a person is vulnerable, sceptical and unhappy or open, cheerful and approachable—even if you don't like to think that's so, it is!

What value does the art of reading faces have today, when ostensibly everything can be explained and analysed in detail? In my view it is even more important! Because we supposedly know all about the world we live in, we have forgotten how to make time for ourselves, to discover ourselves. How often do we look ourselves helplessly in the face and ask: What's the matter with you? And—What happens now? Are the dark shadows under our eyes just the result of a long night—or is there perhaps something more serious behind them? We actually notice the signs, but we do not take the time to look for the cause.

We should realise that everything is written in the face. We have only to summon the determination—and the courage—to have a good look at these signs.

Anyone who has really got to know themselves will also be able to form more meaningful and more satisfactory relationships with friends, colleagues and partners; they will get on better with other people and be able to view their problems with more understanding.

With this book, in which I have restricted myself to looking at those aspects which are of importance in our Western culture, I can give you an insight into the Far Eastern art of reading faces. However, I would like to make it very clear that no one should take the statements in this book as carved in stone. Each of us must take responsibility for ourselves. Our basic character traits are actually already established through our main facial features, but it is the way we handle these predispositions that provides the key not only to our happiness and success but also to our fate. For fate is not just a question of personal predispositions, but also of the ability to make use of chances and exploit one's own potential.

No one is obliged to believe in the wisdom of *Siang Mien*, but it is definitely worth a try!

1

Individual Facial Features and Their Characteristics

Facial proportions

Just as there are ideal proportions for a person's entire body, so there are for the face; in other words, all lengths and breadths can be divided by a particular measurement. For the face this is the width of the eyes.

If you look at the drawing overleaf you will see an absolutely evenly proportioned face, symmetrical in its longer axis. The individual elements match each other in size, location and distribution. The height of the forehead (about twice the distance between the eyes) is the same as the length of the nose from the brows and the length from the tip of the nose to the chin. The distance between the eyes corresponds to the breadth of the eyes and is the same as the distance between the chin and the lower lip and from the lower lip to the nose. This measurement can be found all over the face.

The drawing cannot be classified specifically as either a man's face or a woman's. The facial proportions are the same for both sexes.

In addition the face appears singularly expressionless. That is the result of the symmetry of the shape. There are very few people with a completely regular face. It is the differences in ideal proportions which produce the individual face.

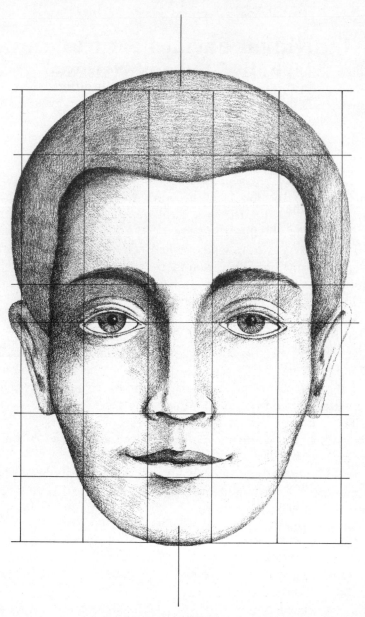

Facial proportions

Face Shapes

Many faces can be classified at a glance as certain typical shapes, whilst others combine features from different shapes. This means that characteristics are mingled when elements of shapes are mixed together. The art of reading faces consists in taking all the features combined in the face as a whole and weighing up which traits have a formative influence on the person concerned.

As well as the shape of the face—which we shall examine in detail in the following pages—the colour of the complexion and the bone structure are important features for interpretation.

A distinctive bony structure to the face indicates that this person can behave very harshly and ruthlessly both to himself and to others. That doesn't mean that he is anything like the violent hero of the Kung-Fu films. It is simply that in his philosophy of life there is very little room for bubbling over with *joie de vivre* or other spontaneous cheerfulness. That doesn't make it easy to establish close contact with him. But we do seek direct contact with people of this type because we instinctively feel that we can trust them. Perhaps that is why they are often burdened with too much responsibility, which they can only cope with by making a superhuman effort, sometimes greater than they need. Anyone who regards such people as perfect can take comfort from the knowledge that they may occasionally suffer from an overweening self-importance and be completely lacking in self-criticism.

A fleshy face structure is the epitome of the hedonist. This type likes an easy life, creature comforts and pleasures of all kinds, and tends to have a predilection for sweet things. The hedonist spends life striving to acquire knowledge and for this reason is likely to develop a particular talent for showbusiness or the fashion industry.

Fleshy-faced optimists would find it unthinkable to reveal their frustration to anybody; they would rather swallow it and put on an incredibly charming smile. They are past masters at disposing of problems: everything has to be as easy-going as possible. So it often seems to us that people like this are to be envied for their insouciance, and we feel strongly attracted to them. They are extremely amusing to be with—so long as they are the centre of attention. But if they feel they are being edged out, they regard this as disrespectful and appear insulted.

According to the Chinese art of interpretation, the colour of the complexion serves as a barometer, allowing us to read a person's immediate state of health and general constitution.

Anyone with a rosy facial skin well supplied with blood automatically radiates a positive approach to life. The character of such people is affectionate and sometimes even romantic. Attractive people are drawn to them as if by magic, and the prospect of new erotic terrain to conquer drives them on to highly imaginative flights of fancy. As soon as their interest flags, rosy-faced people go off in search of new conquests. That does not mean that they are thoughtless, they are simply nervous of committing themselves.

When living with someone else, rosy-faced people are extremely easy-going and will always try to avoid quarrels and find a reasonable compromise. By nature they are highly intelligent, and they go to endless trouble to further their knowledge. It is therefore no surprise that you come across them particularly frequently on in-service training courses and in bookshops.

At first glance a reddish complexion tells us that this person either gets out of breath after any exertion or possibly suffers from high blood pressure.

In reading a face we must be tactful when investigating the reasons for redness of the complexion. Some very active, energetic people easily change and become bad-tempered, even aggressive, in stressful situations. They love their independence, and if someone gets too close to them they can quickly become impatient or unfriendly and blow their top at the slightest excuse. Their ruddy complexion leads one to assume that they enjoy being out in the open air. Physical exercise has a settling effect on their nervous energy: that is why they are so often found out jogging or digging the garden.

A darker but frequently wan complexion leads us to conclude immediately that a person is pessimistic. This impression is not often wrong, because people of this type frequently take life too seriously. They are virtually predestined for an artistic calling because they have been provided with antennae which are highly sensitive to extreme stimuli. Their intelligence does not allow them to take things as they are; instead they will brood over problems night after night. Although their serious nature prevents them from being frivolous, they are undoubtedly interested in sex and amorous adventures, and have shown themselves to be very imaginative and ready to experiment in this area.

It is typical of this type to flit from one subject or field of work to the next. Nothing bores them more than routine.

That is all we need say about these very easy-to-read, general features of the face. Let us now turn to typical face shapes.

Moon face

People with large, round heads can expect harmony and happiness in the family from middle age onwards. Lots of children and a large, extended family guarantee that they will be cared for in the bosom of their family and respected in their old age.

But this is true only to a limited extent if the large, round head sits on a small neck. In this case we must take account of chronic, but fortunately not serious, health problems. Minor physical ailments are also likely.

People with a round face often give the impression of lethargy, passivity and little elegance. Their innate idleness will hardly lead them to high-class sporting achievements. Reluctance to indulge in physical activity stands in the way of common sense. They find much more satisfaction in eating

Male Moon face

Female Moon face

and drinking. We should not be surprised that most victims of useless diets (usually women) are represented here. Their indulgence in over-eating poses the threat of an uncontrolled increase in weight, leading to obesity.

Their skill in dealing with other people and their pleasant manner make them born diplomats. They are regarded as being particularly clever. Serious problems will not be seen as the end of the world, but as an interesting diversion. Although they are good speakers and know how to argue, they often fail to win their case simply because their knowledge is not sound enough.

At work male Moon faces are considered to be smart businessmen. With their wide-ranging knowledge and interests, in their youth they flit from one job and field of interest to the next. Above all they loathe and despise monotony— sometimes it even makes them really aggressive. Their commercial skill does not materialise until they are about 34 years old. They rarely get involved in risky speculation, since they are by nature extremely sceptical. However, quick business deals with solid profits are typical of them, because long negotiations are simply too boring.

At work female Moon faces demonstrate a certain carelessness. They frequently forget to look after their own interests because they are too busy to think about them. For that reason female Moon faces are more often found in middle management than in the executive suite.

In private, Moon faces tend to enjoy one thing above all else: the single life. The fact that most—whether male or female—do not get married until they are in their forties is not actually because they simply ignored the opposite sex in their youth. Rather, for a relationship to continue it must remain interesting and lively. Diversity—and that includes in bed—is everything to them.

Neither sex is at all averse to the occasional affair. But once they have finally made the effort, they head straight for the registry office. And because their sex life is so good, they frequently have a lot of children. There's no need for me to impress on these children how fortunate they are to have a Moon face parent.

Metal face

Siang Mien recognises two types of Metal face. The one seen most frequently has a short face with very full cheeks. What is immediately recognisable in most people of this type is their sympathetic aura. Their health is rather precarious and they tend to have stomach problems.

Those with the long type of face are tall, often over six feet. Very often they are extremely self-centred and inflexible. But they can look forward to a long life.

In general the Metal face is the type most frequently seen. People of this type—both male and female—understand better than anyone how to disguise their feelings by appearing severe. Their intellect, coupled with their pragmatism, can easily result in the selfish accomplishment of their goal. However, they run the risk of a tendency to greed appearing in later years.

These people have a definite predisposition to solitariness — unless they find someone of exactly the same mind. Then we get a look at the other side of their character, the extrovert side.

Metal faces possess a pronounced sense of justice and will defend with great passion what they believe to be right. Perhaps they will even play a little on this characteristic. They like nothing more than surprises, and like to surprise themselves. They can even find great pleasure in entertaining a hand-picked audience with a taste of their humour.

Metal faces are certainly highly intelligent, but they often allow themselves to be led simply by their instinct. Fate seems to take a hand in the way these people fall on their feet time and again—either because they suddenly excel at the head of a company or because they accumulate financial riches quite

Male Metal face

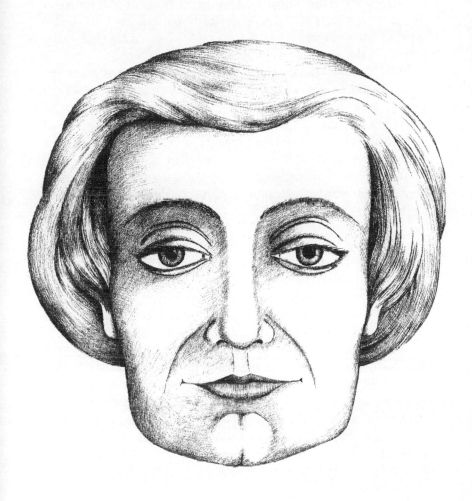

Female Metal face

unexpectedly. They know how to invest without risk by trusting their instincts. A leaning towards politics or law is also
typical: an above-average number of Metal faces are to be
found on the judge's bench or in parliament.

In private, both male and female Metal faces cherish the
more exquisite pleasures of life. If they see an object they
desire, they display unbelievable energy and imagination to
get it. Once they do, however, they will go off in search of
new attractions. This can lead to tension in relationships, which
as a rule prove to be less permanent than expected.

Should Metal faces get married—if they do it at all, they
do it several times—it is quite natural for them to have a lover
as well as a spouse.

Jade face and Wood face

The Jade face, which has a very expressive, elegantly proportioned and rounded shape in the cheek area, is the most
common for the female face. Women with Jade faces have a
mysterious aura and appear very attractive. It is no surprise if
a woman like this has more than one bathroom at her disposal—for they set great store by their image, beauty and
aesthetic sense.

Jade faces—not just the women, but the men as well—have
often had a difficult childhood. But one should not let oneself
be taken in by their delicate façade: they are tougher than they
look, possessing an enormous determination to succeed and a
phenomenal memory.

These people have a very optimistic attitude to life and are
exceptionally quick to display their enthusiasm. Yet they can
be disconcerting because of their sheer vanity. They themselves often have a problem with these mood swings.
Occasional tactlessness or other thoughtless actions can also
threaten their achievements.

A special feeling for the occult and the supernatural is attri-

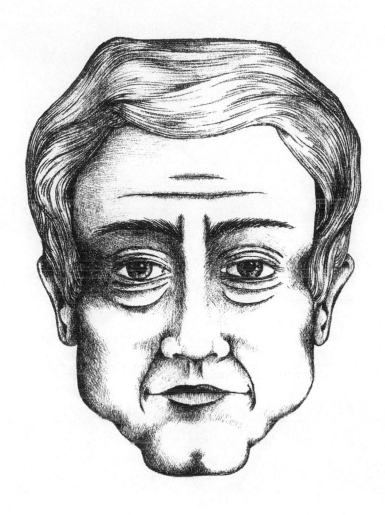

Wood face

Jade face

buted to Jade faces by *Siang Mien*. Their interest in such phenomena, however, is rather more scientifically based.

Women with Jade faces frequently rise to the highest social levels through their determined efforts to achieve success. Because of this, they will often be unfairly condemned as arrogant and unscrupulous.

At work, Jade faces do not allow themselves to become discouraged by great difficulties, thanks to their capacity for energy. They apply their intelligence to the advancement of their careers in such a focused way that they give the impression that they are endowed with a special hunting instinct.

Men with Jade faces often have a tendency to chauvinism. They show a profound dislike for routine. They should, therefore, look for the sort of career that stimulates them and does not easily bore them. A larger than average number are to be found in the armed forces.

All women with Jade faces also need a very challenging profession—they would not want to be sitting in the boss's chair just because of their good looks. The coolness which is often associated with these good looks will be counterbalanced on the one hand by a surprising amount of oversensitivity and on the other by exciting sensuality.

In a love relationship they make the same high demands of their partner as they do of themselves. And if their demanding erotic needs are not fulfilled they are quick to show their disappointment.

These characteristics also apply to Wood faces, whose contours are more marked and more angular and are found—unlike the Jade face—more often in men than in women.

Bucket or Water face

The Bucket face, also known as the Water face, is marked by a broad forehead and a pronounced eye area, immediately indicative of the energy that this person possesses. This very

Male Bucket face

Female Bucket face

respectable character spends virtually his whole life in the pursuit of knowledge. This can be in the most diverse areas: computer technology exercises the same fascination for the Bucket face as does the art of knitting.

People of this type succeed with the help of their intelligence and so earn the respect they deserve. But Bucket faces will also have to live through periods of melancholy and depression, which will dramatically reduce their achievements. One should, however, be wary of trying to cheer them up and of trying to make them snap out of this negative mood—it will not work.

It is often hard for men with this type of face to bring themselves to look into their inner world. Getting close to them and winning their trust can be a very lengthy undertaking. Although he has many friends, the Bucket face often feels that he is basically alone. It is likely that his wavering nature bears much of the blame for this.

The Bucket face is probably unsuited to all work of a routine nature, because he is capable of introducing many ideas of his own. In men with a Bucket face their inherent craftsman's skills frequently conflict with their inability to capitalise on them. But that is by no means the end of the world, since this very original and imaginative character is particularly successful in jobs working with other people or with animals—for example on a farm.

Women with a Bucket face are inherently creative. If this natural talent is used correctly, they can carve out a career on the stage or in the circus.

Bucket faces have many tempestuous affairs, and fall deeply and passionately in love, because their lives would not be complete without physical love. The only threat to their amorous forays is that any serious relationship which develops may come to nothing. For often they cannot distinguish real feelings from a passing fancy.

Fire face

The Fire face, often also referred to, rather scathingly, as an Egghead, has a broad forehead, high cheek bones and a small pointed chin. The intelligence of Fire faces is outstanding and impressive, and they are very flexible. They constantly bubble over with ideas—which they can also from time to time transform into action. But they must work hard to succeed.

In spite of many positive tendencies, Fire faces always make friends with the wrong people because they readily allow themselves to be dazzled by outward appearances where feelings are concerned. But more serious is their tendency to shameless exaggeration. They often get so carried away by their own dramatics that they can hardly distinguish between appearance and reality. It is due just as much to their fate as to their deep-seated mistrust that this type is frequently left to live alone.

Fire faces are of quick intelligence, and sometimes unscrupulous in their striving for power. Their career is mapped out in their youth, but experience shows that it doesn't usually last long. This is because their attempts to trick other people all too often go completely wrong. But this will be balanced by an outstanding talent for observation, which Fire faces, if they are intelligent, use in their work.

Fire faces will rarely have problems in revealing their feelings and desires when they are in love. So this hypersensitive character always finds it utterly incomprehensible that only other people live in happy long-term relationships. If they are completely honest with themselves, however, they must admit that they scare off their lovers time after time because they are so suspicious and have their own problems with entering into a deep relationship. The Fire face must therefore cope more often than other types of face with serious misfortunes in love. The best they can hope for is that their lover will leave quietly and without fuss.

Female Fire face

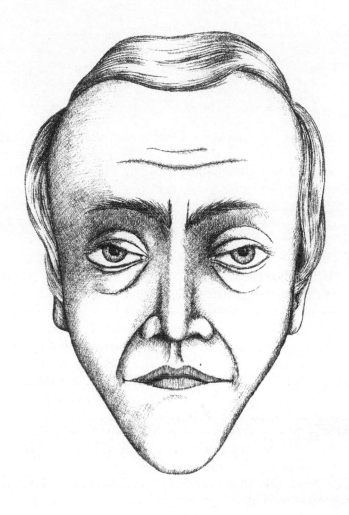

Male Fire face

King's face or Sun face

The King's face, also known as the Sun face, is angular in structure: forehead, cheeks and jawline are strongly defined. This type of face is commonly thought of as being the aesthetic ideal.

Even though this sounds quite unregal, the King's face type is a passionate club freak in private life. For which other type combines all the right qualities for gathering people around and putting leadership skills to the test? With their great success it is hardly noticeable that King's faces are surrounded predominantly by yes-men; for they are so self-satisfied that they have great difficulty coping with opposition.

So little seems to go wrong in the lives of King's faces—both men and women—that one would think there was witchcraft involved. But perhaps they understand better than others how to use their wonderful insouciance to reach for the stars.

King's faces exert an almost magical force of attraction over other people, thanks to their spontaneity and capacity for enthusiasm, and give the impression that they know how to have a great time. But in case so much happiness appears unfair, the fact is that real friendship often remains just an unfulfilled dream for the King's face.

At work, the natural authority of King's faces will make it easy for them to assume a position of leadership. No one will be allowed to share in their success.

The possibility that they might not succeed seems totally foreign to those of this type. Though if they feel that their involvement is not being sufficiently appreciated (financially) at any time, the King's face will soon decide to throw it all in without warning.

It is almost impossible to convince an amorous adventurer like a King's face that love and fidelity have anything in common. Although the passionate King is above all the perfect lover, it is unlikely that a relationship will lead to the registry

Male King's face

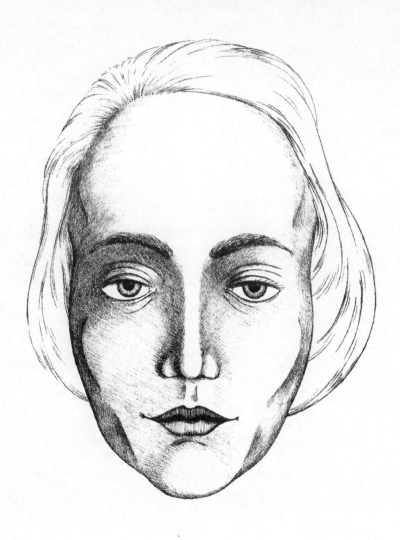

Female King's face

office. He (or she) will be lucky to find a partner who manages to worship him as he deserves. But seriously, it would simply be naïve to expect a King's face to forgo amorous infidelities in a permanent relationship.

Earth face and Mountain face

The Earth face is distinguished by the expressive musculature of the face. Although the forehead is relatively narrow, the chin area is broad and angular. The cheek bones are pronounced.

Earth faces are characterised by a somewhat chaotic appearance—hardly surprising since they have often experienced difficulties in their youth, growing up, perhaps, in a home without love. Since lack of respect is the worst thing that can happen to them, they react violently to problems, sometimes even excessively so: with insults and abuse, often asserting their presumed rights with brute force. Unfortunately they have not learnt to build up friendships either.

A more positive aspect of the Earth face's character is their great thirst for knowledge and their ability to wait until they are given a real chance. Earth faces will dedicate their great potential for energy solely to achieving power. Their thirst for action does not correspond naturally with striving for a career, but rather with a certain bossiness and self centredness.

The career of a female Earth face progresses in a comparatively positive manner. Her round-the-clock commitment results particularly from the desire to acquire a good reputation through being financially secure. But nobody can say that she is not seriously convinced that she has earned this reputation honestly.

The relationship of Earth faces with their partners can be described as highly explosive. Violent disagreements are the order of the day. They only remain bearable if the partner acquiesces in all the decisions the Earth face makes. But if two Earth faces fall in love, they can change the world. They

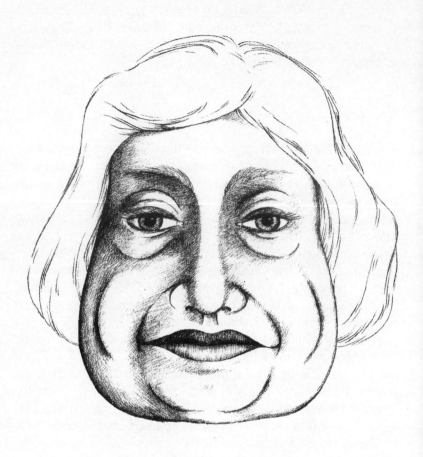

Female Earth face

Male Earth face

will take infinite pains over their mutual promotion—and presumably also manage to bring it about. If one examines a *nouveau riche* family more closely, it can be a good thing to have to deal with two Earth faces.

The Mountain face looks different from the Earth face essentially in its extremely narrow forehead area. The jaw region is approximately as well-developed as that of the Earth face.

Common to both types are a less-than-pleasant adolescence, difficulties in the family and a certain inability to make friends.

Mountain faces can develop quite positive sides if they are accepted for their essential features. They need to be respected and valued for their achievements and one should certainly be wary of serious criticism of a Mountain face: their aggressiveness knows no bounds and is directed at one and all. Mountain faces are very rarely found socialising—not just because they prefer to be alone, but also because it is contrary to their nature to be at the centre of things or to gossip about trivialities. At work the Mountain face is subject to the same fate as the Earth face.

Mountain faces will only enter into a relationship if it promises them a guaranteed financial prosperity, however unromantic that may sound. Their constant striving for power and for a life free from worry needs to be endorsed by their partner. If Earth faces know they have someone standing behind them, they will do their utmost to safeguard the happiness of their private life and that of their surprisingly large horde of children.

Wall face

In the Wall face the distance from the forehead to the chin is extremely short, but the face is wide and stocky. Wall faces are down to earth and can work hard when they need to. But their characteristic awkwardness can also find expression quite often in laziness and a certain anxiety. For example, when

Mountain face

Wall face

faced with serious difficulties it sometimes happens that they lose control because of their inherent mistrust of things—and, in the worst cases, their behaviour becomes intolerable.

Typically this person lacks the ability to put existing ideas into practice. Perhaps this is due to the Wall face's inclination to search continually for the ultimate proof of his or her ability. So as not to undermine their self-confidence, one should refrain as far as possible from criticising Wall faces—there is not a shred of evidence anyway to suggest that they will benefit from such criticism.

Wall faces have absolutely no use for authority, either exerting it or putting up with it. Since they have a fairly fickle nature it remains doubtful whether any success at work will be permanent. But should Wall faces for some reason come to recognise their creative abilities, they could cause a sensation as a media star, or at least become reasonably well-known.

On the other hand, anyone who expects discipline and far-sightedness from Wall faces will be bitterly disappointed. For there is a constant danger of them suddenly throwing in the towel and walking away.

The reason why Wall faces stumble from one private catastrophe to the next probably lies in their inability to express their feelings. Since they will have nothing to do with red roses and promises of undying love, conflict in partnerships is difficult to resolve. People of this type will always have a tendency to bewail their fate bitterly to another lover, rather than trying to salvage their existing relationship.

Those who want to cope with a Wall face will have to face the fact that their love life will be rather conservative and that their erotic dreams may well be smashed to pieces.

The asymmetrical face

Most people have several asymmetrical facial features. An irregularly-formed nose, for example, is very common, and in the Chinese system of interpreting faces this is considered to be a sign of emotional weakness. However, one very rarely comes across total asymmetry: either one half of the face is longer and/or broader than the other, or the mouth is lopsided, or the nose is crooked.

If possible one should steer clear of people with obviously asymmetrical faces because, according to *Siang Mien*, this appearance does not augur well. Particularly when the features lead one to conclude that the external irregularity mirrors an internal irregularity.

Clearly, the asymmetrical face often exerts a great deal of fascination. It appears to radiate an aura of extravagance. However, on looking more carefully, this can turn out to be an attempt to distract from mediocrity.

However, no one should assume that people with asymmetrical faces are stupid. They are past masters of all the tricks needed to use others for their own ends and can be very unforgiving, even vindictive, if anyone thinks they are being unfair. It is very likely that people with irregular faces will be career-minded and in later years will amass a substantial nest-egg.

As far as work is concerned, those with irregular faces will do well, above all in areas where their infallible empathy for everything new can profitably be used, for example, in journalism or market research. A certain amount of stress and action will not harm them: they know how to channel their generous supply of physical energy in the right direction. But one should avoid overloading people with asymmetrical faces with responsibility or tying them down too hard. They will use their disarming charm to extricate themselves and leave it to others to put their mistakes right.

Asymmetrical face

Asymmetrical faces have a strongly developed emotional life and can be incredibly considerate, affectionate and easy-going, even if they themselves get a raw deal. It is apparent from the way in which they throw themselves into amorous adventures that love is their favourite hobby. A relationship quickly becomes the focal point of their life. As does the next one, and the next one. For no one knows better than asymmetrical faces themselves that they are not at all suited to marriage.

Forehead

The forehead not only affects the visual appearance of a face, it is also a kind of display window for thoughts and intelligence. For a more precise interpretation *Siang Mien* subdivides the forehead region into three levels, each of which embodies a different aspect of the human spirit.

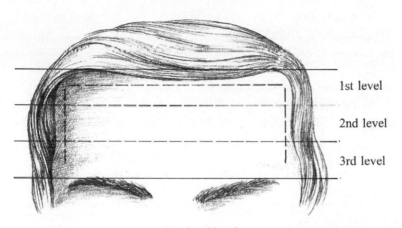

1st level

2nd level

3rd level

Forehead levels

In the Chinese art of reading faces the first level is known as the *celestial region*. It reflects a person's intelligence and his or her capacity for logical thought as a gift bestowed by God. What individuals make of this gift will determine their fate in the future.

The second level is the *human region*. It contains the memories that people have amassed as a result of their upbringing and their experiences. The moral standards they have acquired are also reflected here.

And lastly, the third level is the *earthly region*. This is the seat of all intuition resulting from experience.

Together these three regions represent fixed periods of time in one's life: the celestial region the first 30 years of life, the human region the period between 30 and 60 years of age and the earthly region the last phase of life.

It is said that the first wrinkles appear after the first 30 years. These too are important signs. Chinese tradition considers two or three horizontal wrinkles on the forehead to be an indication of happiness. If one particular wrinkle occurs quite high up, it will be seen as a sign of intellectual ability. A wrinkle occurring lower down is taken to be indicative of restricted spiritual activity.

However, the general composition of the three regions is more important. They may be smooth and flat or well-developed and domed. The ideal forehead can be described as smooth, with all three levels equally domed and generous in height as well as in breadth. A good forehead is worth as much as having a good sum of money to fall back on.

In the following pages, as well as the different forehead shapes, we shall examine the most distinctive forms of hairline since the hairline is an extension of the forehead. *Siang Mien* talks about an infinite number of hairline variations. We shall look more closely at the five most important variants.

Broad forehead

If the forehead is broad, it is assumed that a correspondingly broad spectrum of knowledge is concealed behind it. A person with this characteristic has no qualms about showing his or her forehead to anyone, for someone with a quick intellect will not hesitate to take on challenges.

The mental and spiritual values of broad forehead people are quite striking. Such people stand up unflinchingly for their own and other people's rights. Their rhetorical skills and their talent for adapting instantly to each new situation come in very useful here. When it comes to uncovering the truth they can sometimes be extremely unreasonable and will not shy away from the consequences, however unpalatable. Yet it cannot be said that, in their enthusiasm, they ever forget the good upbringing they have received.

It is worth looking in particular at the broad forehead with a low-lying hairline. We are dealing here with a theoretician, who can only rarely use his or her knowledge for any practical

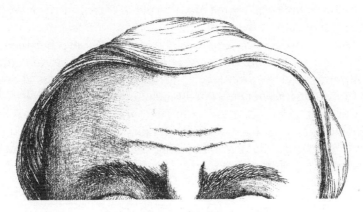

Broad forehead

Broad forehead with low hairline

purposes. In extreme cases this type of person may be idle, lacking in energy and even stupid. Sometimes such individuals are completely devoid of any sense of justice as well.

People of this type are often burdened by fate with a family which demands an incredible amount of spiritual and financial support. They feel that unfair demands are frequently being made on them and this contributes to the bitterness in their nature. This is, perhaps, the basis for the moody side of their character, while its negative aura further reinforces their pathological mistrust.

This is made even worse when the low-lying hairline is combined with a broad but shallow forehead. This indicates symptoms such as emotional and financial meanness as well as those negative tendencies already referred to.

But that does not mean that everyone with a low-lying hairline has to put up with such an unhappy fate: these people are of a practical nature and can lay the foundations of a good life with their inherent handicraft skills.

Narrowing forehead

Siang Mien regards this type of forehead as very unfavourable. The narrow forehead indicates narrow-mindedness and pessimism. A tendency to intellectual and emotional chaos seems

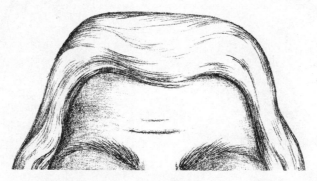

Narrowing forehead

to have been with such muddle-heads from the cradle. Their judgement is inadequate, their behaviour less than prudent. Possibly these people are the ones who suffer most from this burden—which would also explain why people with this type of forehead have so little confidence in themselves.

A more positive combination is represented by a narrowing forehead combined with a high hairline. At least then there is a certain amount of intelligence behind it. An obvious example of this is the so-called Egghead, who battles through life with wit and charm.

High forehead narrowing to a point

At its best, a forehead like this also has a high hairline and appears smooth and well formed. It indicates great intelligence, carefulness and decisive behaviour.

Experience shows that there is usually quite a capable person behind this type of lofty brow. It is a type very often found in scientists and scholars.

People with a forehead like this will usually only be per-

High forehead narrowing to a point

suaded to take decisions after thorough consideration. Their ability simply to ignore the unimportant makes it easy for them to reach the right decision in most circumstances.

People with high foreheads are actually rather eccentric at times, but they are quite open-minded and have a marked tolerance towards their fellow human beings.

Low forehead

A low forehead indicates a childhood and adolescence beset by problems and conflicts. It may be an advantage for these people to realise as early as possible that they cannot rely on others for help.

Their basically conservative upbringing means that they are frequently too traditional and they therefore find it difficult to accept anything new.

At times they also find it difficult to talk about their feelings. It is more appropriate for such people to communicate in writing.

Their modesty and their ability to make the best of a given situation and accept the limits of possibility can prove to be very positive. Their sense of reality protects them from becoming profoundly disillusioned.

Low forehead

Flat or concave forehead

People with flat foreheads have difficulty making decisions. They are hesitant characters whose tendency to set up in business on their own implies a great deal of risk. On the other hand it is also difficult for them to accept orders from superiors. Their permanent know-it-all attitude and a tendency to interfere in anything and everything often make them individualists. It therefore follows that people with flat or concave foreheads vacillate a lot in their moral ideas.

These negative aspects mean that someone with a flat forehead is not particularly lovable. But should these people manage to convert their enviable imagination and ideas into deeds, then their success is assured!

Flat forehead

Concave forehead

Smooth or rounded forehead

According to Chinese interpretation the most favourable type of forehead is in general smooth or rounded. This type indicates clear thinking, intelligence and the courage to behave resolutely. People in this category have the amazing knack of being in the right place at the right time. They are adaptable and flexible, but do not get bogged down in unacceptable compromises. However, there is always the danger that they will allow themselves to be dazzled by their own brilliance, resulting in a certain arrogance.

People with this type of forehead rarely need to worry about failure in either their private life or their work. All the more so since, thanks to their flexibility, they are receptive to everything that is new, and it would never occur to them to rest on their laurels.

Smooth forehead

Rounded forehead

Arched hairline

A hairline like this might suggest a whole host of excellent qualities, but above all it indicates a person motivated purely by economic considerations. These characters are suited above all to positions of leadership in the business world, thanks to their good judgement and work ethic.

People with an arched hairline are often famous, or sometimes even infamous—either way they are exceptionally successful. They are the sort of people who are actually able to reflect on their success, but this hardly ever happens because they are permanently striving to reach new goals. Their peaceful nature lends them a certain unconventionality, and this allows them to bring fairness and understanding to their dealings with their colleagues and subordinates.

All this is true for women as well as for men. Women with arched hairlines are also frequently found in positions of leadership. They too have a definite tendency to independence at work.

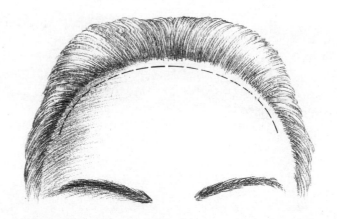

Arched hairline

V-shaped hairline (widow's peak)

Tradition, agility, instinct—these often inherently limited gifts appear to dominate the lives of people with a V-shaped hairline. Because of their conventional upbringing they fit into a hierarchy without any difficulty. This makes it particularly easy for them to find acceptance in many areas of life—and also in many professions.

But these people can easily fritter away their money, because they are rather unsettled and tend to do several things at once. However, this in no way affects their efforts to accumulate money.

Women with a V-shaped hairline sometimes have difficulty in harmonising their goals and their feelings. Perhaps this is one reason why they often seem to be so set on confrontation.

Without a doubt, both sexes have a great deal of eroticism and sensuality. At least, their charisma would seem to indicate these qualities. Men with this kind of hairline often display many feminine characteristics, but this in no way detracts from their masculinity.

According to *Siang Mien*, the first couple of years of married

V-shaped hairline

life can be like a horror film for women of this type. They have been brought up to accept the traditional woman's role but find it difficult to follow in practice. However, if this phase can be weathered without too much psychological damage, the marriage will last.

M-shaped hairline

People with an M-shaped hairline rarely have any ambition for positions of power at work. They are far more likely to find fulfilment in creativity. Should these people pursue a career in the arts—for example, as actors, visual artists or writers—astuteness and philosophical interests will bolster their career.

Their sensitive, affectionately tender character makes these people outstanding lovers.

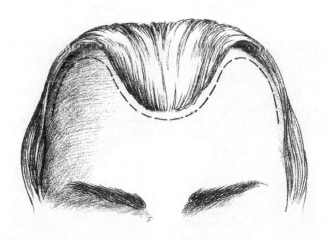

M-shaped hairline

Triple-curve hairline

This hairline is not so widespread—fortunately, one might perhaps say. For the predictions connected with it are extremely unfavourable.

A great deal of effort and iron discipline are needed, particularly with regard to themselves, by people with a triple-curve hairline if they are to achieve even a satisfactory standard of living. The probability is that they will suffer health problems from the age of about 30, just as they will inevitably have to work hard physically to attain a comfortable lifestyle.

Square hairline

A square hairline is found predominantly in men and only very rarely in women. Reliability and thoroughness are the hallmarks of this character, and a tendency to maintain close contact with their family throughout their life.

At work they instinctively prefer any activity in which they

Triple-curve hairline

have to follow orders. If, contrary to expectations, they want to make a career for themselves, there is always an expectation in the background that they will be suitably rewarded. If recognition is not forthcoming, then these people's energy easily turns to depression.

There is an old Chinese maxim that might have been coined especially with people with a square hairline in mind: Change your hairstyle, and you will change your fate for the better.

Square hairline

Eyebrows

Our glance at people's eyebrows will tell us a lot about their general constitution, their present state of health, and their hopes and goals. It will also tell us how they are going about reaching these goals—whether their path is direct and focused on their goal or stressful and strewn with obstacles.

The shape of the brows and the angle between them are as important for a reading as the distance between them. For example, the distance between the eyebrows can tell an experienced observer about a person's energy level and also about the degree of attraction—including sexual—that that person exerts. The eyebrows are just like the eyes—a mirror of inner harmony, displaying a person's intentions, energy, ability to act and decisiveness.

Perfect eyebrows are as rare as perfect facial features. They are frequently asymmetrical. If the left eyebrow is a little more powerful than the right, then one can infer an enormous ability to assert oneself. If, on the other hand, the right eyebrow is more marked, that particular person much prefers to put off making decisions.

According to Chinese interpretation, a pessimistic and stubborn character lurks behind very short eyebrows—regardless of their shape, thickness or colour—for this is someone who was not exactly overwhelmed with love as a child. Experience shows that such people lurch from one crisis to another with quite fateful regularity, and indeed, the prospect of an early death cannot be ruled out.

If the brows are very long we are usually in the company of a friendly, winning person whose longing for love and security can inspire a protective instinct. These personalities have difficulty severing their ties with the parental home, so such sensitive people will certainly have relationship problems.

If—and this is about as likely as getting all six numbers in the Lottery—both brows are absolutely identical in shape and proportion, glossy and strong (the distance between the eyes and the centre of the brows is ideally the width of a finger laid flat between them) then this person will be 'upright and wise', according to *Siang Mien*.

Before you can read the eyebrows, you must be sure of their original shape. This is particularly true of women who, for reasons of fashion, pluck, tint or paint their eyebrows. People also try—mostly subconsciously—to alter their personality by altering the eyebrows: certain character features will be concealed and others emphasised. It is interesting that in some cases the outer change actually mirrors an inner change: self-confidence will be increased, which will lead to stabilisation of inner harmony.

Eyebrows also give an indication of the state of health. For example, the underlying cause of hair falling out of the brows is frequently a disturbance in the function of the kidneys.

Thin eyebrows

Thin eyebrows represent discipline and order. Often, clinging firmly to principles and rules can become an obsession for a person with thin eyebrows and then every positive step forward means five steps backwards.

These people seem quite disaster-prone, but their problems are intensified because they prefer to look the other way when conflicts arise. At best they will not despair completely, but

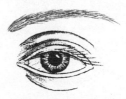

Thin eyebrows

rather recognise that their obsession with criticism and their high-handedness are the cause of their difficulties.

That does not mean that people with thin eyebrows have no real chance in life. Success in middle age—mostly between the ages of 35 and 40—indicates that they have a great deal of ability and a sense of order.

Things take a turn for the better when they discover that others are willing to return their smile. These people are happy in a steady relationship and have a particular talent for family life. But they may sometimes find it difficult to feel enthusiastic about sex.

Women with thin eyebrows who use make up to thicken them should not rely too much on the eyebrow-pencil-inspired self-confidence saving them from life's pitfalls.

Thick eyebrows

People with thick eyebrows are generous and very emotional. They definitely have a tendency to fool around, but they are also drawn to action and adventure. They are able to use new ideas spontaneously for their own advancement. But their perseverance is not up to much, simply because they hate life's trivia.

Their career will often have been mapped out in their youth, but later on they will give it up without a second thought in favour of other interests. People with thick eyebrows appear

Thick eyebrows

to produce good ideas as if from a production line—and from time to time they even have the patience to convert them into action.

This type is passionately, enthusiastically and incessantly in search of security. But in reality they hardly ever have a permanent relationship with a partner.

Women who pluck thick eyebrows do this purely for cosmetic reasons. Their lives are happy enough without any correction at all.

People with extremely dark thick eyebrows enjoy excellent health, according to the Chinese interpretation.

Close-set eyebrows

A short space between the eyebrows indicates personalities that are spontaneous and inclined to volatility. Their very superior manner may turn out to be a sham, an attempt to conceal their own uncertainty. But they are positive characters who always respond to challenges. They believe unshakeably that they can achieve everything—and against all the odds, it does appear that this is what frequently happens.

They react to relationships with partners in a rather less positive manner. There is always the threat that their underlying jealousy will bring them more sorrow than love.

Close-set eyebrows

Wide-set eyebrows

A larger space between the eyebrows is a sign of hesitancy. These characters, endowed with enviable patience, need to do little in order to be loved by everyone. Because of their patience and sensitivity they are eminently suited to social commitment.

But these people will only manage to assert themselves in exceptional cases. Their greatest weakness is a lack of self-confidence. Even when they manage to rise to a high position at work success is still not certain. But once they are conscious of this they have quite good career prospects.

In their private life, these people frequently turn to an association or some other group which is most in keeping with their feelings or which they instinctively feel will most easily compensate for their uncertainty.

People with wide-set eyebrows often long for a genuine partnership, but more often than not they are inhibited and shy away from sex.

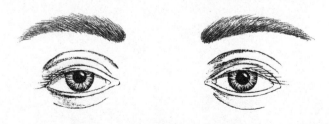

Wide-set eyebrows

Eyebrows that meet

According to Chinese tradition, brows that meet herald considerable problems. As a rule we are dealing with a character with a very sensitive nature, in whose presence we frequently feel guilty, because such people are very quickly offended and take everything unnecessarily to heart. All their lives they are capable of being hurt by what they see as an insult—even if it is only imagined. These people have a clear tendency to suffer from depression, which on closer examination isn't really justified. In extreme cases they retreat within themselves and this leads to long-term psychosomatic illnesses.

Even when all these less than positive tendencies are present, they do not necessarily have to become a burden. Career opportunities frequently become apparent from the age of 35 onwards. The pleasure that this person derives from competition at a time of career advancement is amazing.

Men with eyebrows that meet will have had to rely on the uncompromising support of their partner, since without this support their strength could quickly steer them in the wrong direction. A striking feature of women with this type of eyebrows is their tendency to end their career abruptly, and take refuge in home and hearth, if their partner gives them the slightest chance of doing so.

Eyebrows that meet

Eyebrows that shoot straight up from the base

In *Siang Mien*, this eyebrow shape is always an indication of an adolescence beset by problems. But negative experiences in the parental home could actually have a positive effect— if these people have learnt not to rely on others.

The energy they bring to any situation which will work to their advantage has to be admired. But from the age of about 34 they may also have to go through periods of despair, simply because they seem to lack that little bit of luck which, in their view, they deserve. But the prognosis for these people is optimistic: there is a good chance that their hard-won success will be permanent.

A partnership with someone with eyebrows like this may well turn out to be very positive, because they will value love and affection precisely because of their harsh experiences and will be able to satisfy even the most secret desires as a potent and uninhibited lover.

According to Chinese tradition, if these people suddenly lose hair from their eyebrows, they will lose a brother or a sister before very long.

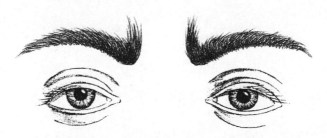

Eyebrows that shoot straight up from the base

New-moon eyebrows

Eyebrows that are evenly curved in the shape of a new moon are found predominantly in women. They reflect balance and harmony as well as an assured elegance. There is no doubt that these carefree, usually attractive people know how to arouse the sympathy of their fellow human beings.

Presenting themselves well professionally will rarely be a problem, as shown by the high proportion of people with new-moon eyebrows who work in the media.

Both men and women of this type will be dominated by their sexuality. In their youth, erotic desires might easily degenerate into an obsession with sex, and in extreme cases could even assume the characteristics of an addiction. *Siang Mien* tells us that the danger of this is particularly great when the brows are very dark.

In their private life people with new-moon eyebrows know how to value the good life: pleasant surroundings and a partner who shares their sensual interests.

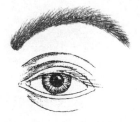

New-moon eyebrows

Triangular or knife-shaped eyebrows

People with triangular or knife-shaped eyebrows are very astute, full of energy and hungry for power. Although in their youth they are more concerned with physical activities and social involvement, later on their interests turn towards things which are rather more intellectual and spiritual.

Excessive energy may be the driving force behind their need to be in the limelight and their tendency to extreme exaggeration. This restless energy is also frequently the reason for a fanatical love of gambling.

But under no circumstances should one forget the other side of this agile character—that is, their sensitive, sympathetic and extremely charming traits. Their ability to communicate and their erotic flair make those with knife-shaped eyebrows particularly popular with the opposite sex.

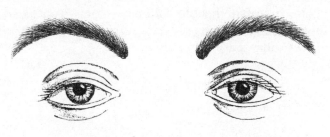

Triangular eyebrows

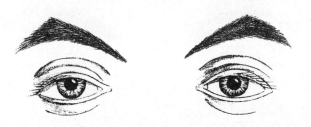

Knife-shaped eyebrows

Men of this type have a constant appetite for sex, something which might prove to be an obstacle in the way of a stable relationship.

According to the Chinese interpretation, women with knife-shaped eyebrows prefer the role of big sister to that of passionate bedmate. It is easier to satisfy their needs by leading them onto the dance floor than into bed.

Unruly eyebrows

Eyebrows that look messy usually belong to people with chaotic minds. They find it as difficult to marshal their thoughts as to adapt themselves to other people. In extreme cases they have a tendency to be very tactless.

Between the ages of 30 and 35 such people often indulge in yearning and daydreaming, but these are illusory from the outset. Nevertheless, they often succeed in bringing method into their life. When they do, success comes their way.

Women will try to impose some sort of order on men with unruly eyebrows. This will have a positive influence on their self-confidence.

Women with this type of eyebrows will generally prove not to be chaotic in relationships with a partner. They can be very gentle and constructive, provided that they meet a partner who gives them security and encouragement.

Unruly eyebrows

However, their male counterparts will have to work hard for their happiness. It will be observed that they instinctively turn to domineering and/or older women, from whom they hope to gain support and guidance.

Curly eyebrows

Eyebrows like this also indicate unsystematic thinking and behaviour. These people are generally clever but egotistical, and are in a position to work systematically for the goals they set themselves in their career. This is how they consistently, sometimes even downright unscrupulously, satisfy their lust for power. More often than not, their career will gain momentum from the age of 30.

In their private life, people with curly eyebrows often suffer from an inability to love. In their search for happiness they may stumble from one amorous adventure to the next. For them a stable relationship is the exception rather than the rule.

Women with curly eyebrows are much less affected by this. For example, they will be amazingly successful in committing themselves to family and partner and in achieving their need for fulfilment in marriage.

Curly eyebrows

Straight eyebrows

This type of eyebrows signifies someone who is physically healthy and of a practical turn of mind. According to *Siang Mien*, the straighter the brows, the more down-to-earth and straightforward a person is.

Imagination and imaginativeness are not generally among their strengths. But their pragmatism and unshakeable optimism will more than compensate for this shortcoming. They have clear goals, they follow them consistently, and they achieve them most of the time. Minor setbacks rarely dampen their spirits, for they possess good humour in abundance.

It is likely that they will also find other people's financial worries amusing. Thanks to their excellent instinct for making large profits, they themselves will never be in financial difficulty. This applies particularly to men with straight eyebrows who, once they have reached a position of power, will fight tooth and nail to maintain it.

In relationships with partners, men and women with straight eyebrows behave in quite different ways. Whilst a man can turn out to be really happy-go-lucky when in love, a woman will strive single-mindedly for a lasting relationship. But it should not need emphasising that no sexual acrobatics can be expected from her in the bedroom.

Straight eyebrows

Upward-sloping eyebrows

In the Chinese art of reading faces these are considered to be particularly auspicious. Obstacles seem not to exist for these personalities. They do of course—but such people simply ignore them.

Although one gets the impression that fate has smiled on those with this type of eyebrows, they work very hard for their success—and not at the expense of others.

But they also have weaknesses: they start many things without finishing them, because they get impatient and lose interest halfway through.

In a personal relationship there will be no lack of exciting interludes. But the partner who overestimates the placid nature of this character may get a nasty shock: behind that gentle exterior lurks a will of iron.

The evidence of *Siang Mien* is not quite so positive about people with upward-sloping eyebrows that are broom-shaped. They should not rely too much on good luck: fate could one day show them its unfriendly side.

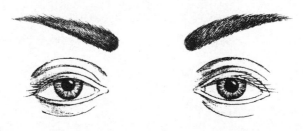

Upward-sloping eyebrows

Downward-sloping eyebrows

This shape of eyebrows indicates a lack both of ambition and of determination to get the most out of life.

But one cannot assume from this that these people get nothing off the ground. If they concentrate, they can transform their aggressive tendencies into positive dynamism and will inevitably be successful.

Setbacks at work in their early thirties are not unusual, which means they must be particularly mindful of the threat of financial losses. But these setbacks shouldn't be a reason to panic, for experience shows that from the age of 37 their career really gathers momentum.

In general, downward-sloping brows indicate a tendency to melancholy, which can intensify and become depression. If this tendency exists, experience shows that matters come to a head between the ages of 30 and 35.

As a rule people with eyebrows like this are very trusting and extremely shy. For that reason there may be difficulties with a partner at the beginning of a relationship, particularly in the sexual sphere. But this should not discourage their partners: the refreshing honesty of these people does at least offset their rather negative qualities.

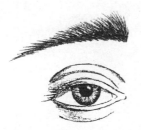 

Downward-sloping eyebrows

Other eyebrow types

Besides the shapes of eyebrows mentioned, which are the most common, I shall give brief descriptions of some others:

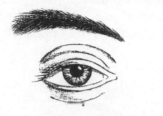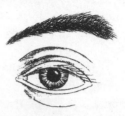

Eyebrows with pointed inner ends
Not readily assertive, indecisive, great need for
security, very family-orientated.

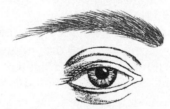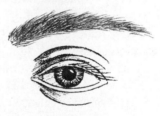

Long eyebrows
Sensitive to beauty and aesthetics, thoughtful, behaves uncertainly and
hesitantly, good sense of family.

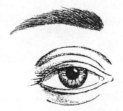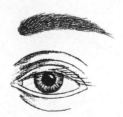

Very short eyebrows
Easily hurt, passionate, often capricious, strong feelings,
behaves emotionally.

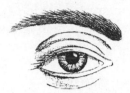

Eyebrows low over the eyes
Extremely ambitious, aggressive, tendency towards curiosity, great
persuasiveness, all-round interests.

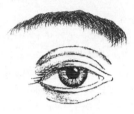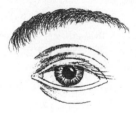

Eyebrow hairs curved downwards
Aggressive nature with a tendency to pessimistic low-points, creative
life-style, but not easily capable of inspiration.

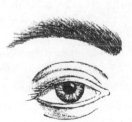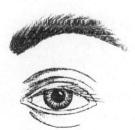

One eyebrow higher than the other
Suffers from mood swings, tradition-conscious, sensitive, easily
hurt.

Eyes

The eyes are perhaps the most important element in a person's face. Not just because we pick up optical stimuli and impressions through them, but also because in them we are able to read the fundamentals of facial interpretation.

The Chinese art of reading faces regards the eyes as the seat of the soul. They represent the direct entrance to a person's inner being, to his or her character, emotions and attitudes. It might well be possible, with a great deal of effort, to practise a particular facial expression, but the eyes cannot dissemble. They give the lie to the facial expression and reflect a person's true self.

Siang Mien doesn't just interpret the shape of the eyes but also takes account of the whites. Above all it examines the state of health. Thus it is well known that a rather yellow tinge indicates that the individual may be suffering from jaundice or some disease of the liver. Bloodshot whites give grounds for assuming that a person is aggressive and therefore inclined to 'see red' when angry.

The size of the white of the eye is also important: if it appears larger than the iris, it indicates an apathetic, inflexible personality with an impoverished emotional life. Women will also be assumed to be unresponsive in bed, perhaps one of the reasons they frequently have problems with their fertility, and sometimes even remain childless.

From the medical point of view other features which need to be interpreted are the dark rims of the eyes (they frequently indicate heart or gallbladder problems) and the lower lids if they are dark or have just a blackish tinge (this often means that the bladder or kidneys are at risk).

Last but of course not least, *Siang Mien* considers the colour of the iris. As a general rule: dark eyes cheerfully take responsibility for their families and make sacrifices for them. But a Chinese proverb states: If a woman has eyes as brown as tea she is very open and easy. The darker her eyes, the more

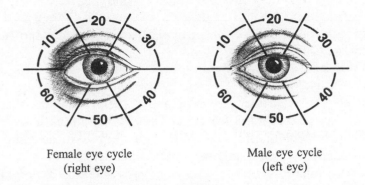

Female eye cycle
(right eye)

Male eye cycle
(left eye)

hungry for sex the woman is. Light-coloured eyes mean that she loves to be sociable; but her common sense and egotism mean there is little room for feelings.

Most people use intuition and their personal experience of life to interpret the actual expression of the eyes, for example their lustre and a person's totally individual, direct gaze. The Asian interpretation of faces, on the other hand, obtains the essential information from the anatomy of the eye.

It should be mentioned briefly that the Chinese art of reading faces also infers information about the individual phases of life from particular segments of the eye. That is too detailed to be gone into here. Let us just say that the eye is divided up into segments in accordance with a 60-year life cycle. In women the right eye is used, whilst in men it is the left eye.

Large eyes

Large eyes epitomise the ideal of beauty. They are considered to represent intelligence, strength, a person teeming with ideas and a sincere character.

It is no secret that people with large eyes have tremendous sex appeal. Being aware of their erotic charisma, people with large eyes tend to be aroused quickly—and their feelings tend to subside again to normal levels just as quickly. Women with large eyes are thought to be particularly experienced playmates who are willing to experiment.

Men and women with large eyes evince a great deal of warmth and sincerity for their fellow human beings, but on the other hand they become extremely vulnerable should something not go according to plan. Their biggest plus must be their extrovert, unaffected nature. And they have absolutely no inhibitions about making a grand entrance.

In their careers, people with large eyes will stop at nothing to be in the limelight. And where better could they satisfy this need than in showbusiness, advertising or in the media and the arts?

Women place great reliance on the fact that a big-eyed look has the advantage of boosting their career—anyone who experiments with this will rarely be disappointed.

The same qualities that are attributed to people with large eyes are often found in people with round eyes. There is no

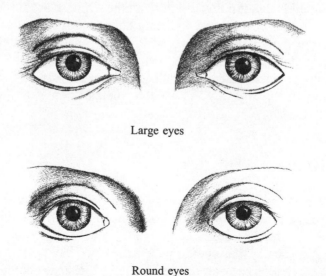

Large eyes

Round eyes

need to point out that women who have eyes that are both large *and* round have an absolutely irresistible effect upon their fellow human beings—and not just from an erotic point of view.

Small eyes

Eyes which are noticeably small are taken to be a sign of jealousy, unreliability, and stubbornness. From time to time people with this type of eyes turn out to be real villains.

However, one should be extremely careful about adopting such negative opinions. It is easy to assume that people with small eyes have negative personalities, because nothing and no one is allowed to come near them or their private space.

According to *Siang Mien*, people with small eyes are loyal and extremely pernickety. Professionally this is not necessarily a disadvantage. They are, moreover, extremely goal-orientated and dedicated in their aims. But they quickly lose patience and may, if they feel they are being ignored, torment their colleagues with all kinds of trivial fault-finding.

In a relationship people with small eyes always strive to provide their partners with every conceivable luxury. But their pig-headedness and jealousy will prove to be the death of the relationship in the long run.

Their attention to detail can be useful in areas of work where this is important. So, for example, one frequently finds men

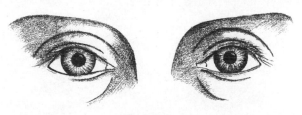

Small eyes

with small eyes in the accounts department or in an organisational role.

Women, on the other hand, need an audience in order to be happy in their work. So they turn to jobs in the fashion world or in journalism. Unlike many of their own sex, they appear to be positive and prepared to take risks. Their career prospects are brilliant. For in spite of their unsympathetic and know-all manner and their tendency to be dogmatic, it cannot be denied that people with small eyes are very intelligent.

Upward-slanting eyes

In the Chinese art of reading faces this eye shape is also regarded as the ideal of beauty. It indicates an emotional person who is blessed with intellectual perspicacity and a wonderful constitution. But above all this type possesses the gift of enjoying life.

In dealing with people like this one must be prepared for occasional outbursts of sudden rage. To make matters worse, they frequently direct these tantrums towards those who are closest to them.

For this reason there is always the threat that a relationship with a partner will break up quickly and without good cause.

Women with eyes that slant upwards are very hesitant where love is concerned, and are easily influenced by a third party. It is quite possible that they despair of their own doubts; their partner often takes to his heels because he gives up when faced with the fickleness of his doe-eyed beauty.

Upward-slanting eyes

In business people with eyes of this type are flexible, sure in their decisions and able to tackle problems promptly. They will not shy away from hard physical work either, provided that a job promises variety and constant challenges. Both sexes can count on successes at work which are thoroughly deserved. However, work can try their patience somewhat because their career only really starts to gain momentum after the age of 35.

Downward-slanting eyes

In Japan eyes of this shape are considered to be a symbol above all of great good luck and wealth. In the West, eyes that slant down are associated with gentleness, helpfulness and trust, but also with a tendency to melancholy.

For these people deep and sincere friendships will be the source of strength for a life which, though often full of self-sacrifice, is still satisfying. These noble-minded characters seem predestined to help others out of the most terrible troubles, but it would never occur to them to blow their own trumpet about their good deeds. This sort of person just listens—and keeps quiet.

Anyone who envies so much gentleness and understanding should realise that people with this ideal type of helping nature not only have to put up with fewer of the low points in life than others, they also have fewer of the high points to enjoy.

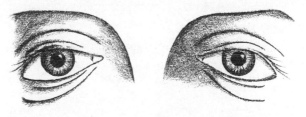

Downward-slanting eyes

Women with eyes like this usually have a good instinct for well-heeled men and will know how to assess financial advantages. But one should not assume that the material aspect of life is a priority with them.

In love they can be very conformist and devoted, to such an extent that they not only allow their partner to dominate them but are actually happy in this role.

It is more the exception than the rule for some women with downward-slanting eyes to wind their lovers round their little fingers. It should be less of a surprise that they will be good mothers.

In the world of work these people are employed almost without exception in nursing or social services, which may best correspond to their natural disposition. No other profession offers so much scope to make the most of their characteristics.

Men with eyes of this type are also able to develop sound commercial skills, which, if directed in the right way, will enable them to run a profitable business.

Close-set eyes

People with close-set eyes often have a very calculating nature and tend to be introverted and, at worst, narrow-minded.

Obviously they are not often aware of these characteristics themselves. For they appear to like to be more dynamic and sociable than their character would suggest.

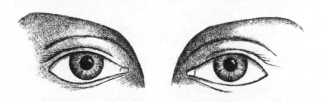

Close-set eyes

In reading the faces of people with eyes of this type one should take particular care to include all their other characteristics. For *Siang Mien* also interprets close-set eyes as a sign of good temperament, sociability and the clever assessment of advantages.

People who possess these essentially positive qualities can easily be sensationally successful at work. They may be best suited to politics and commerce, because they can develop the ability to adapt quickly to new situations and exploit them to their own advantage.

Women whose eyes are this shape have much more complicated characters. They appear to move from one problem to the next with the greatest of ease. Perhaps their, to put it mildly, outsize curiosity is to blame for this. It is not surprising that their assumption that they are superior to everybody and everything, and that they have nothing more to prove, makes their fellow human beings doubt their credibility. Often these archetypal women find that love proves to be a story without a happy ending, perhaps because it is expecting too much of them to enter into a permanent relationship on the basis of mutual trust.

At work a certain timidity about taking risks could have a negative effect on the career of these women. For promotion remains the exception rather than the rule, even though they appear to establish themselves particularly quickly in a job.

Wide-set eyes

These eyes indicate openness, courage to face life and other positive tendencies. People with wide-set eyes normally have high expectations, but occasionally they seem to lack that little bit of dynamism needed to achieve them. In their dealings with others they sometimes prove downright naïve, their outsize credulity accounting for a great many human disappointments.

Wide-set eyes

Setbacks of this kind can cause a complete emotional upheaval, leading to serious mood swings.

Their unstable psyche can have a very detrimental effect on these people's performance at work. So this type is not usually suited to a career that demands dedication.

Both men and women with wide-set eyes can expect happiness in a relationship with a partner. If they find a suitable mate they may find themselves living a really sensational love story.

Deep-set eyes

These eyes generally belong to a pensive and deeply romantic personality. But let no one be deceived by that mysterious romantic air: fortunately, these people do not lose their sense of reality either in their actions or their feelings.

Something in their nature seems to demand that in their youth they undertake their own personal odyssey—at work as well as in love. They do not concentrate on promotion until their late thirties, when the wealth of experience they have accumulated can prove to be very useful.

They could write novels about love, so numerous are the love affairs that they have usually enjoyed. These experiences provide a firm foundation for a strong relationship in which they can be really fantastic partners.

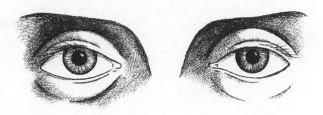

Deep-set eyes

Protruding eyes

The Chinese art of reading faces has very few complimentary things to say about people who have protruding eyeballs. These people are thought to be extremely egotistical and untrustworthy, though they are also perspicacious and strong-willed.

The combination of these attributes often makes such characters particularly successful. All the more so since they have no scruples about getting involved in a somewhat shady deal if it promises to make them a quick buck. But not all people with protruding eyes are wicked profiteers—often it is only the envy of their fellow men which gives rise to this image.

People of this type often stand out because of their panicky

Protruding eyes

behaviour. This may be a sign that they have been beset by problems from their earliest years—for instance, a parental home where there was not enough love or understanding.

Men frequently have a very marked sexual appetite and will try anything to satisfy it. They are unable to shake off their egotism, even during the act of love, and so they rarely enjoy a permanent relationship.

Women with eyes of this type frequently appear slightly naïve. They are always at risk of being taken in by so-called friends, and at worst may even stray from the straight and narrow. Their egotism is less conspicuous, but shows itself in a tendency to change partners rapidly.

Triangular eyes

People with triangular eyes will be aware that others don't particularly like them. This could be partly due to the fact that they dislike arguments and therefore have a tendency to impose their own views on their fellow men or to manipulate them. They have difficulty in opening up to other people, so any attempt to communicate with them will be nipped in the bud.

In their early years they show little staying power at work and are in the habit of starting a lot of things without actually finishing anything. Yet they are versatile and would be suited to a variety of occupations. For example, people with eyes of this shape have an aptitude for a political career.

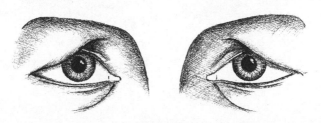

Triangular eyes

Their relationships with partners, too, are fraught with obstacles. As a rule they show just as little staying power here as in their job. They may embark on a relationship or marriage with the best of intentions, but there is a very real danger that it will end in separation or divorce. Nevertheless, they appear to have no lack of deep and genuine feelings.

Rectangular eyes

This eye shape is often found in highly intelligent people who work with their minds. Nothing escapes these interesting characters and they can quickly see through the façade of others. But their intelligence will often get in the way—above all in their search for personal happiness.

The need for security runs through their life like a *leitmotif.* This is particularly true of their careers. People with rectangular eyes are commonly found in administrative jobs, many as civil servants.

In private life too security is their prime motive. They are likely to go into a relationship not so much out of overwhelming passion, but more as result of very careful consideration. This type is not often in a position really to enjoy sex, because they seem to be inhibited by an instinctive block against sensual action. Yet as a rule a relationship with a partner will be permanent because no sexual frustration appears to exist after 20 years of marriage.

Rectangular eyes

New-moon eyes

In China they say that eyes shaped like the new moon are a sign of even greater dishonesty than a fox's eyes. In our culture they are not exactly considered beautiful, but these people are mostly kind and easy to please. For this reason they have a very equable temperament.

Men with eyes of this shape may be inclined to cheat anyone they consider inferior—though if anyone should get wise to this they will most probably back down quickly. In the workplace, on the other hand, they are generally easy to deal with—due rather less to their character than to the fact that a power struggle would simply be asking too much of them. People with new-moon eyes usually have no difficulty in establishing themselves in a big company, although their hopes of reaching the top are unlikely to be realistic.

Falling in love may be somewhat problematical for this type. Trying everything out—fine. But in a stable relationship they feel the threat of getting out of their depth.

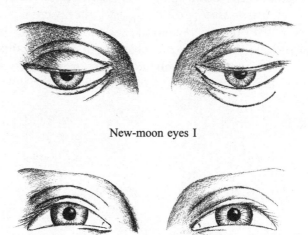

New-moon eyes I

New-moon eyes II

Other eye shapes

There are numerous other eye shapes, which can only briefly be touched on:

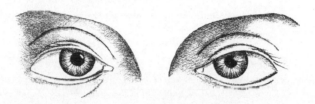

Crossed eyes
Introverted and shy, impatient, little stamina, possesses a
strong will to live.

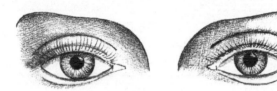

Eyelashes curling up
Optimistic, very sensual, temperamental, strong
feelings, constantly needs new challenges.

Sly look
Frequently self-centred, mistrustful, unreasonably jealous,
has a great deal of imagination.

Sleepy look
Little self-confidence, low expectations, often resigned to
disappointment, dreamy, phlegmatic.

Lewd look
Adaptable, idle, often content to go along with the crowd,
rarely capable of taking the initiative, lacking in concentration.

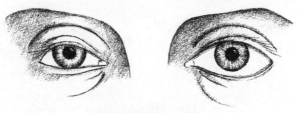

Non-matching eyes
Needs to be appreciated, ambitious, sometimes stubborn,
expects a great deal of others, highly imaginative.

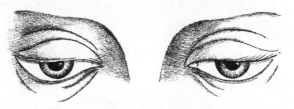

Dragon-shaped eyes
Magnetic personality, quick-witted, soft-hearted, says
little about him- or herself.

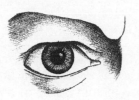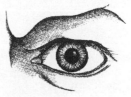

Imperious look
Energetic, cool, frequently dissatisfied, has an enormous thirst for action.

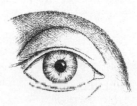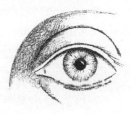

Piercing look
Unscrupulous, astute, highly intelligent, good judgement.

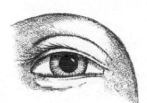

Sensual look
Strongly magnetic, intensely emotional, all-round
interests, tends towards a luxurious life-style.

Nose

The Chinese consider the nose to be a gauge of wealth and importance. For this reason they also describe it as an economic treasure. But it is also used as a measure of a person's vitality and sexual powers. It is generally agreed that the nose tells us everything about our fellow human beings' intellect, knowledge and ability to love. It is worth considering just how many catch phrases are connected with this sense organ: to have a good nose, to have a nose for something—and many more. The nose is also important as a bridge between the eyes and the mouth—*Siang Mien* even calls it the 'centre of life'.

In the following pages we shall concentrate on the various shapes of the olfactory organ. But we shall also have to take other factors into account.

For example, the colour is also informative. A pale pink nose is associated with happiness and inner harmony. If the nose is a bright red, that indicates joylessness and a violent temper—or excessive consumption of alcohol. The Chinese are well aware that a red-nosed person is not always a drinker—but that he will always be called one.

The Chinese art of reading faces also studies the shininess of the nose. Before you place any bets, you should make sure that your nose is shining. Then, so they say, you can count on winning money.

The shape and size of the nostrils also have significance. According to *Siang Mien*, broad nostrils indicate good fortune in financial matters, whereas narrow ones point to a spiteful personality in which the nostrils are pinched together resentfully.

The art of reading faces also has something to say about the tip of the nose. If it is broad, then financially the person in question is set up for life.

The groove, the indentation which runs from below the nostrils down the middle of the upper lip, also has to be considered. In Chinese tradition this is called the 'channel of the feelings'. People with a marked groove are considered to be emotional and receptive to sensual pleasure. A weakly formed groove, on the other hand, is a sign of chastity and repressed desire.

Straight nose with straight tip

A straight nose not only presents a pleasant appearance, it also combines clear thinking, tolerance and trustworthiness with unyielding tenacity.

Almost without exception, it is outward appearances that matter most to people with this type of nose, and being true aesthetes they take a great deal of care stage-managing their entrances. They are also likely to be great experts on the subject of art and beauty. For these people, an elevated social position and faultless manners appear to be just as important as careful cultivation of their own positive image.

One of the less pleasant features exhibited by this character is a certain superciliousness and a tendency to look down on other people who are less fortunate. This streak of vanity can come to the fore especially when people with straight noses have made it in life, either at work or in their private lives.

In matters of the heart these people do not find it easy to make decisions. For this reason they may risk getting involved in three-way affairs.

It is no exaggeration to describe men with this type of nose as snobs in relationships with a partner. They usually demand the highest standards of their partner, and it would be a dream come true if she boasted a royal title. Should their expectations be unfulfilled, these supermen are inclined to satisfy their sexual needs with pornographic magazines.

Women are also very wrapped up in themselves, and their vanity shows itself in its worst light in matters of love. Before they will allow a man into their bedroom they will thoroughly examine his social and financial background. Only when this

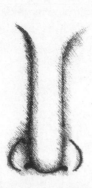

Straight nose with straight tip   Straight nose

process has been favourably concluded will they be ready to smile at him in a gentle, seductive manner.

Careerwise, people with straight noses have little need to worry. In areas where it is important to make a good impression and promote their business, these clever people can climb all the way up to the top. Men of this type are often found in the media, at the head of a company or in artistic occupations. Women are able to make a career for themselves as personal assistants or gliding along the catwalk as a model. But they can often be found in the role of housewife—with a cottage in the country, of course.

Roman nose

This nose is long and has a downward-sloping tip. It symbolises courage, including the courage to attack—for Roman warriors, who were known to be very brave and always ready for battle, had noses like these—and also a well-developed ability to make decisions and think clearly.

People with this kind of nose seem to be ready for heroic

action in this day and age, too. They are very ambitious, delight in every kind of challenge and can achieve great prosperity in middle age.

On the work front, they can often reach high positions in commerce or science, sometimes in the armed forces as well. They are considered to be cool, calculating people and are very skilful at keeping a poker face during business negotiations. This cool reserve will carn them the respect of their colleagues. This is the basis for their power at work.

People with Roman noses are rarely known for hiding their light under a bushel, but it would not be quite accurate to describe them as show-offs. They seem much more interested in the rewards that promotion brings: financial security and all the comforts that go with it.

Women with this type of nose are likely to have a large appetite for sexual adventure. They seem insatiable in this respect and need little persuading to fulfil their lover's weirdest requests.

What men with Roman noses need most from their relationship with a partner is challenge. If their thirst for sexual conquest is satisfied too quickly, their lust for a particular woman may easily fade.

Roman nose

According to Chinese interpretation, people with a Roman nose are considered unreliable and cold if the tip of the nose slopes sharply downwards.

The smaller the nostrils, the more likely it is that such a person will take risks. At the same time they show incredible self-confidence—and actually end up on the winning side most of the time.

Hooked nose

Anyone with a hooked nose—also called an Indian nose—usually has an infallible instinct for money and business, whether it be on the Stock Exchange, in real estate or in banking. As a rule these people are completely wrapped up in their work and are able to call on great physical and emotional reserves in their quest for success.

People with hooked noses are not only hungry for success, but are also always on the look-out for financial advantage—and they find it. It is extremely likely that they will arouse envy, even resentment, in their colleagues at work.

Although money seems to open doors everywhere, they do not always achieve social acceptance. Who would really want to surround themselves with such narrow-minded people—at least officially? This may be the one problem that people with a hooked nose are unable to solve—one which runs through their whole life like a *leitmotif*.

In their working life, women with this type of nose may develop outstanding educational abilities as well as commercial instincts. For this reason a career as a teacher, coach or consultant is quite on the cards.

Men with hooked noses sometimes reveal extremely excessive sexual tendencies in their youth, while at the same time searching for a partner whose physical needs correspond with theirs. These men can be very generous when they are in love. But when their feelings fade, this generosity usually comes to an end. As they grow older their sex drive reverts to normal and they come to value the worth of real love and spiritual harmony more and more.

Snub nose

A snub nose is a small nose sloping upwards at the tip, so that the nostrils are usually clearly visible. People with this pert nose shape frequently lack spiritual and physical maturity. It indicates moodiness and temper, but also sensitivity and generosity.

Such people appear to know everybody and everything, but they are so carefree that they get into all kinds of trouble. In their work this unpredictability may occasionally take on an almost self-destructive aspect.

Any dreams of quick promotion are completely illusory. In fact, some snub noses are able to accumulate a great deal of money in their youth (for example, in fashion or in show-business), but their lack of staying power and concentration

Hooked nose

Snub nose

means they run the risk of losing just as quickly all that they have achieved. Sometimes their weakness of will can have quite a different basis: they simply don't like doing anything unless they have to.

Other people will be captivated by these personalities, partly because of the naïve charm they radiate. If everything is going well, they are liable to be just as unhesitatingly generous with their affections as they are with their money.

When people with snub noses are in love, they want to see their dream fantasies realised and to enjoy them with complete abandon. So it is typical of them to strive unconsciously to boost their own ego. Should they fail in this, they may have no problem in dispensing with sexual desire altogether.

Fleshy nose

People with a fleshy nose—the majority of whom are men—are generous, emotional and sensitive, but also sensible enough not to get involved in speculation. Success will rarely be handed to them on a plate; instead they will have to fight hard for any promotion. But then, most of them are fighters from

Fleshy nose

a very early age anyway, because, although they appear to be very family-orientated, in their youth they were frequently forced to stand on their own two feet.

In their private life people with this type of nose tend to help others, even if they have to make many sacrifices themselves. At the same time, curiously enough, they find it incredibly difficult to show their own feelings.

By and large their life will be positive, with a permanent upward trend. This means they will only be happy if they can finish what they have begun. In any case, being happy is far more important to them than financial wealth. Perhaps that is one of the reasons why people with fleshy noses seem so well balanced.

Women with this kind of nose may develop great skill in the sphere of home economics, so they are often found in professions connected with this—for example, in hotel management.

Men with fleshy noses have problems with their sexuality. One would think that with their vulnerable personality they would be sensitive lovers. The fact that they are not is perhaps due to their inability to put their feelings into words. Until they finally find the courage to whisper their love, they will be unable to fan the flames of love in the lady of their heart. If failures of this sort pile up, there is a danger that these men will increasingly cool off and, by the time they are 40 or 50, will have learnt to ignore their feelings completely. They will then sublimate their erotic needs in their working life.

Bumpy nose

A bumpy nose symbolises an outwardly strong but stubborn character of rigid opinions which he is very reluctant to change. But this strength is only for show, a fact indicated by the way this type all too quickly becomes unsure.

These people can be very generous—not least to themselves—and are frequently regarded as experts in the art of living. If they ever let their tendency to a vagabond life surface, they will find it hard to stay in one particular place.

In their career they are in danger of being rash or hasty. If success is too long in coming, people with bumpy noses will quickly become impatient and will abandon their job without so much as a by-your-leave, moving on to some other occupation.

A relationship with a partner is worthwhile for men with bumpy noses only as long as it satisfies their pronounced sex drive. Their inability to acquiesce in their partner's needs, other than in exceptional circumstances, proves how difficult it often is for them to make a commitment.

Women run the risk of being unable to free themselves from their prudish habits. When it comes down to it, they can never decide whether to say yes or no.

Bumpy nose

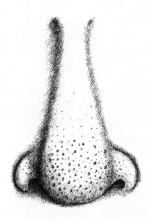

Leonine nose

Leonine nose

The leonine nose is found chiefly in men. Those few women who have an olfactory organ of this type will simply be regarded as ugly.

People with a leonine nose are seriously at risk of psychological weakness. They know how to arouse sympathy and can be the best of friends. But one should never draw attention to particular faults because their worst nightmare is having to stand up to criticism. Fundamentally, however, they are very generous and prepared to take chances. As good speakers and energetic tacticians they can count on rapid promotion.

At work they can very often excel at the head of a company. They have abundant ambition and will not be content to stay in a middle-management position.

These men are also like lions in love: they need a whole harem to keep them happy. If they should risk a stable relationship, they are highly unlikely to make their lover very happy. As a rule, their sensational sexual prowess means they have a lot of children.

If the tip of a leonine nose is unusually red, then according to *Siang Mien* that person is in danger of a heart attack or high blood pressure.

Crooked nose

Fortunately very few of us have a really bent or crooked nose, for *Siang Mien* has little of a positive nature to say about it. People with a nose like this are thought to be weak characters, very unbalanced and moody, and at times quite spiteful.

They have often had little attention from their own families, or have been unable to arouse interest in themselves. It may be that they have become particularly vulnerable as a result of these experiences, a fact they try to conceal by putting on

Crooked nose   Turned-up nose

a show of self-confidence. In spite of their emotional need they will under no circumstances allow others to get close to them. Careful observation of these people will soon show that they are only fooling themselves by putting on an air of optimism.

At work people with crooked noses have a tendency to manipulate their colleagues for their own ends. They are not particularly patient and so their plans often fall through.

In a partnership people with crooked noses are said to have an almost ridiculously trusting nature. They project all their longings and feelings onto their partner and are shattered if a relationship falls apart. But if they meet a partner who also needs a lot of loving and caring and who can above all be tolerant, this relationship will be permanent.

Turned-up nose

The bridge of the nose looks similar to that of a snub nose, but the tip is plump and round. A nose like this symbolises level-headedness, practical thinking, balance and reliability.

People with this kind of nose are the proverbial kindly uncle and aunt. A friend with a turned-up nose can safely be trusted with your most intimate secrets—everything will remain secret. Or you can borrow money from them and it will never occur to them to say no. Someone with a turned-up nose is the sort of person who feels a real need to help others.

Sometimes they can be too good-natured for their own good: they can easily get hurt themselves, through doing so many favours for friends. Not surprisingly, they usually attract a large circle of friends and acquaintances. They can be very entertaining, particularly in company. Because they secretly value being the centre of attention, they will in all modesty enjoy their popularity.

The helpful turned-up noses usually manage to do quite well in their career and in the course of their lifetime can expect to see their wealth increase, provided that they are ready to put in the effort and to take at least a modicum of risk. People with a turned-up nose can be trusted completely in everything they do at work: whatever they start, they will finish.

One should not expect a person with a turned-up nose to be consumed with passion when in love—that really would be asking too much of them. It is much more usual for someone with this type of nose to have a solid relationship. Though once they are sure of their partner, they can develop eroticism through sensuality and a cautious desire.

Other nose types

In addition, the following types of noses are quite frequently to be found:

Flat nose
Manually skilled, entertaining, fundamentally pessimistic in outlook.

Aquiline nose
Cool tactician, business-minded,
aggressive, has considerable stamina.

Narrow nostrils
Self-confident, inclined
to stubbornness, likes to keep
his or her distance, very
vulnerable, interested in
spiritual or highbrow things.

Short nose
Little self-confidence, prefers to
keep options open, liberal,
jealous.

High nose
Artistic understanding, restless,
tendency to solitude, in search of
ideals, vain.

Mouth and Lips

According to *Siang Mien*, the mouth is the most important part of the face apart from the eyes and nose. It reveals essential information about the intellect, feelings, love, personality and health. We are able to communicate verbally with others by means of the mouth, and we can also express pleasure or sadness without words.

The mouth is also one of the centres of our physical desires. It is no wonder, therefore, that those who interpret the face are able to read all sorts of things in it on the subject of love. In China they say that the mouth reflects the sensuality of the female sex. That is why, from time immemorial, young girls have been brought up to keep their lips closed so that they don't reveal their sexuality.

But a Chinese proverb also says, 'Once a word has left our lips, not even the fastest horse will be able to catch up with it.' Which should encourage us to weigh our words carefully before they leave our lips.

In the following pages we shall concentrate primarily on the nature of the lips for our interpretation. As a general rule, the upper lip represents feelings, intellect and passive needs, and the lower lip represents the active expression of individual desires.

In addition, the colour and appearance of the lips are also important when interpreting the face. Delicately radiant lips are always a sign of health and well-being, whereas if they are dull it means that the body is out of balance, and that, for example, organic changes are taking place.

If the lips are a light pink colour one can deduce that this person will not lay claim to any earth-shattering needs, but will be quite modest in his or her demands. If they are red and obviously well supplied with blood, this person is honest, direct, but also quite ambitious. Dark lips indicate a materialistic person with extravagant sexual needs; such a character knows how to control his or her feelings consciously and appears never to lose control of them.

Sex is really important for women with dark lips, but rarely uppermost in their thoughts. They prefer to devote themselves to other qualities—for example, to being a good mother. Very pale lips frequently indicate sexual inhibitions, often even frigidity.

What does the ideal mouth look like? It is well proportioned, has clear outlines and corners that go up. The lips should be neither damp nor dry. The line between the upper and lower lips should be straight.

But the perfect mouth is rarely found, just like other perfect facial features.

Small mouth

People with a small mouth are introverted, strong-willed and charming, characteristics which will help them to get on quite well in life. But sometimes it is the less favourable features that help them to make a sensational career: a large helping of egotism and bossiness.

People with small mouths do not allow difficulties to get them down. Hardly anyone has mastered the art of fighting their way through quite as well as they have. The smaller the mouth, the more likely it is that the most important element of their personality is their determination to assert themselves. These people frequently also have a strong yearning for independence, which can easily make them loners.

They will appear to be loners more often than they them-

Small mouth

selves would like; indeed, they have to be because they are dedicated to criticising everything and everybody. The fact that they can be mercilessly tactless in their criticisms only serves to make their life even more difficult.

In love, women can be quite undemanding and passive partners, becoming pregnant extremely quickly in their youth— provided that they allow themselves to be conquered in the first place. As a rule a husband will live very happily with a woman like this, so long as he can come to terms with the fact that her whole life will be geared to home and family.

A man with a small mouth would definitely have something to say about love, because he can be a controlling but interesting lover who knows how to celebrate sex as an art. Although a relationship with him can be lasting, it depends a great deal on how ready his partner is to fit in with his needs.

Large, full mouth

A large, full mouth looks undoubtedly erotic and, in women who boldly emphasise the shape of their voluptuous lips, it is a sign of bewitching sensuality. Sometimes it also indicates a tendency to frivolity. According to *Siang Mien*, a large, well-delineated mouth is the clearest indication of passion.

These people are also by nature extremely outgoing, and are mainly encountered in business. It is true that they have a tendency to be content with superficial affairs, partly because they seem to be dependent on the constant admiration of others, partly because they are simply incapable of serious relationships.

Large, full mouth

At first glance a full mouth conveys an impression more of appearance than reality. Unfortunately, in most cases closer examination does not reveal any more reality.

People with a voluptuous mouth will inspire their partners erotically time after time. Anyone who knows how to satisfy them in this respect will be surprised by their generosity. Their great egocentricity doesn't allow them to be very expressive, but they can be relied upon to be faithfully passionate.

Upper lip thicker than lower lip

If the upper lip is thicker than the lower one, the Chinese regard it as a sign of insincerity. In Western culture, however, these people are judged much more positively: as emotional, usually very sensual, and very generous to themselves and others. They are also considered to be skilful speakers, who can plead a cause convincingly and well.

The skills which they have at their disposal are important to them, just as the demands they make are unlimited in order that they may achieve a really good quality of life. For as a rule they are confirmed sybarites. Most of them have a weakness for good food and are often wonderful cooks themselves. They also enjoy poetry and other arts. But there is a danger that their imagination, allied with their sense of enjoyment, will get the better of them and throw their sense of reality off balance.

These people appear to take love lightly. They do not brood over problems for a long time and prefer to concentrate on more agreeable matters — love or the art of seduction, for

Upper lip thicker than lower lip

example. And they appear to be past masters at it. No wonder, either, that these people—men as well as women—are thought to be the best lovers, whose partners can hardly complain of a lack of variety.

Lower lip thicker than upper lip

People with a thicker lower lip are not considered to be particularly trustworthy. It may be that a tendency to constant chattering contributes to this image. But their occasional over-estimation of their own abilities also contributes to the fact that people with a thicker lower lip are often denied recognition.

Thanks to their inherent eloquence and quick-wittedness, however, these people have a very good chance in the field of entertainment: it is not difficult for them to amuse their fellow human beings. Their success will continue so long as nobody asks them to work together with others in a team.

Incidentally, 60 per cent of men have a thin upper lip!

Men and women with a thick lower lip appear very sensual and attractive, and they should be able to look back over a long and varied list of affairs. But they sometimes give the impression that they are searching compulsively for love and eroticism. Perhaps that is why they keep forming relationships with partners who appear to be as unlikely to remain faithful as they are themselves.

Lower lip thicker than upper lip

Protruding upper lip

This type of lip is found most frequently in women. These people give an impression of uncertainty and timidity— nobody appears to be as convinced of their own lack of talent as they do.

Their pessimistic self-assessment is no accident. Often this can be traced back to the fact that in their youth they experienced little love and encouragement, and had to put the interests of others before their own.

At work worry about decisions and responsibility may make it almost impossible for them to achieve a position of importance, though they will be happy as a subordinate member of a team.

As far as their health is concerned, people with a protruding upper lip tend to suffer from allergic diseases. It is probable that such illnesses generally have psychological, rather than organic, causes.

Anyone who wants to discuss relationships and sex with these people will come away feeling indignant. For them, love

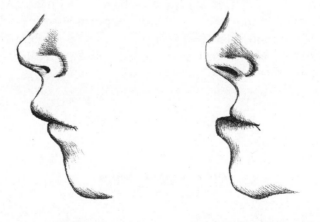

Protruding upper lip   Protruding lower lip

is a taboo subject—though in practice they appear to enjoy it. Bed is the one place where they can throw all their worries overboard and lose themselves completely in their sensuality.

Protruding lower lip

In China a woman with a protruding lower lip doesn't enjoy much of a reputation for sociability: they say that she drags her possessions back into her own home. In our part of the world, however, these people appear to be very warm-hearted and above all free and independent.

They frequently surprise us by being clever business people. Women of this type place less importance on their reputation at work than on the financial rewards by which they can measure success.

On the other hand, men with lips like this are more interested in being the boss in their job. Quite often they will already have had it drummed into them in their youth that they are destined for leadership.

Good behaviour will be just as foreign to people with a protruding lower lip as will any attachment to a particular place or region.

In matters of partner-swapping, too, they tend to be wanderers. They seem to take pleasure in constantly changing partners. Men in particular will sense a threat to their independence should their lover make demands concerning marriage.

In any case, possessiveness in relationships seems to be alien to women with a protruding lower lip. Their world will not collapse if they should discover that their lover is sharing his bed with other women.

Pouting lips

People with pouting lips rarely take the trouble to conceal their vanity and arrogance. And they can hardly complain about being bored either—for they often put themselves under considerable stress to prove to themselves and others how fantastic they are.

People with lips like this are, as a rule, quite open-minded, but one should certainly not expect much intelligence from them. On the other hand, they sometimes have a pronounced artistic talent. Most of them seem to be like an actor who is constantly on stage.

Their dealings with others can sometimes be full of conflict: their self-willed character will only rarely allow them to form an intimate friendship—perhaps because they are afraid of showing their feelings.

In love this type requires a great deal of patience. It takes time to convince themselves that sex is the best trifle in the world. But even though they may still be shy of foreplay, if they once get a taste for it, they will be perfect lovers.

Pouting lips

Straight lips

People with straight lips are said to have a great deal of power, a thirst for knowledge and intelligence. But they are also thought to be tenacious fighters, who will stop at nothing to get their point of view accepted. They will also go all out to pull the wool over other people's eyes if it looks like being to their advantage.

They will always strive for a leading role at work, because it would offend their self-importance if they were asked to do something of little consequence.

In love these people are also ruled by their intellect, although sometimes a proper degree of lasciviousness is added. It may sound illogical, but should their ambitions in this area be satisfied too quickly, they will easily lose interest in sex. In their later years they will come to regard harmony in their relationship with a partner as much more important. In the end, they know that eroticism isn't everything.

Straight lips   Straight line between the lips

Crooked mouth

According to *Siang Mien*, a crooked mouth is a symbol of dishonesty and cunning. The Chinese have a popular saying: 'Crooked mouth—crooked thoughts!' But in this case, when interpreting a face one should first of all carefully take into account all the other characteristics before jumping to any conclusions. For not everyone with a crooked mouth is inevitably a baddy.

There is, however, a tendency in their character to create their own reality and, moreover, to pull others to pieces. Though it would be rather too drastic to describe all these people as potential liars, they do frequently give others that impression. Without doubt, people with a crooked mouth will have to work hard to overcome their unflattering image.

Crooked mouth

Men and women have no real staying power in love and so long-term relationships are rare. They frequently even remain alone all their lives, thanks to the unflattering picture given of their character.

These people may get mixed up in all sorts of adventures in their search for true love. Even three-sided relationships cannot be ruled out. But in the end they will be defeated by the fact that they themselves cannot keep their mouths shut in bed.

Corners of the mouth turned up

Siang Mien says that a mouth whose corners turn up reflects luck. Actually these people look as though they are smiling all the time. Their mouth gives an impression of pleasure and optimism—and to a certain extent this corresponds to the truth.

Anyone who appears to be as happy as this will usually not stay alone for long, for other people feel drawn quite magically to such an air of optimism. However, this can quickly become a burden to those who have a mouth of this type, because the affection that people show them can sometimes assume the proportions of a stranglehold.

People like this seem to be assured of a simple journey

through life, for they have an abundance of imagination and adaptability. Now and then they will shamelessly fall back on a small white lie, if they can turn it to their advantage.

Corners of the mouth turned up

Men whose mouths turn up at the corners are often thought of as playboys—but they are much too harmless to be heartbreakers. On the other hand, their preference for full-bosomed women is beyond dispute.

Women with a mouth like this enjoy passionate lovemaking, most of all in the mornings. They are regarded as active, refined lovers whose life would lose its sparkle without sex. But they can also be very romantic, and if this side of their character has a happy ending they can live a love story straight out of a film.

Corners of the mouth turned down

Anyone who has a mouth like this gives the impression of being bowed down with care and radiates a pessimistic aura, often without realising it. According to *Siang Mien*, people who have a mouth with the corners turned down are liable to have problems with their stomach and their digestion.

These traditionally-minded people appear to be the victims of a complicated fate, particularly in their early years when they can be beset by all sorts of difficulties. As born loners they will fortunately quickly find out that no one is willing to give them encouragement and so they will adapt to the situation.

In spite of their great intelligence they do not appear to think it worthwhile networking in an effort to promote their career. In China they say, 'They do not sing the right tune'. Which in plain English means: these people will have to fight really hard for promotion. Their tendency to speak their mind bluntly can also get in their way.

Corners of the mouth turned down

Happiness in their life will not start to blossom until they are 45, and only then will a love relationship be permanent and the circumstances favourable to bring them fulfilment. For in their younger years the need for sex and for changing partners seems more powerful than the need for a real relationship.

Other mouth types

In addition the following mouth and lip forms can also be found:

Lines running together (convergent)	Lines running apart (divergent)
Strong feelings, passionate, temperamental, very sensitive to the importance of other people.	Disciplined, self-controlled, modest but purposeful, with a thirst for adventure.

Lines parallel
Thoughtful, reliable, attentive to
other people, shies away from risk
and all changes.

Thick lips
Passionate, enthusiastic, very
emotional, weak character,
prepared to take risks.

Wavy line between the lips
Great self-confidence, open-
minded, needs material security,
good speaker, likes to be in the
limelight.

Dimples at the corners of the mouth
Suffers from an inferiority complex,
likes to show off, unforgiving, really
knows how to enjoy life, artistic
talent.

Teeth

In China they believe that not only can you deduce the state of health and constitution from the teeth, but you can also find there indications of a person's development, and, above all, of parental upbringing. But the teeth can also teach us something about relationships with other people.

If people have bad teeth they don't like to show them—for example, they rarely laugh heartily. They say that anyone with bad teeth inevitably also quickly develops complexes and becomes withdrawn and inward-looking. And from time to time such people will be quite dissatisfied with themselves.

But if people have a magnificent set of teeth, perfectly

regular and shining, then their mood and their dealings with others will be characterised by joy and laughter.

In the following pages I shall point out in a shortened form some of the most important characteristics of teeth to which you should pay attention:

Uneven teeth
Compulsive sexual need, moody, tendency to melancholy, starts many things without finishing them.

Long teeth
Indecisive, slow, eloquent, fantastic memory, avoids all risks.

Large front incisors
Stubborn, impatient, very sensual, needs constant recognition from others.

Even teeth
Open, basically optimistic outlook, prepared to take risks, emotional.

Large teeth
Business-minded, has an eye to own interests, always needing new things to do, security-minded, secretly vain.

Small teeth
Tradition-conscious, ambitious, with a tendency to egotism, active, enjoys being self-indulgent.

Gaps between the teeth
No clear sense of direction, frequently
changes opinions, greatest
goal is personal comfort.

Gums visible when laughing
Outgoing, rarely has personal
opinions, anxious, exercises restraint
in all things, obliging.

Protruding teeth
Stubborn, often pig-headed, able
to communicate well, lies for personal
advantage.

Teeth sloping inwards
Thinks and acts unconventionally,
shy, reserved, finds it difficult to
get close to others.

Cheeks

Siang Mien considers cheeks that are in balance with the nose and have a slightly rosy sheen on them to be the ideal. Basically, the Chinese interpret rosy cheeks as holding out a promise of happiness. Well-formed cheeks represent energy, decisiveness, the ability to assert oneself both at work and in private, happiness and will-power.

For example, one can easily tell from the nature of the cheeks how a man's career will develop between the ages of 30 and 45. According to *Siang Mien*, the higher the cheeks, the more promising the career. Anyone who scrutinises the faces of successful entrepreneurs and captains of industry will notice that these people frequently have very well-developed cheek bones. Although in our culture bony cheeks are regarded as particularly attractive and well-favoured, the Chinese masters take a quite different view of things: *Siang Mien* admires rounded cheeks, for they indicate that their owner has greater power than someone with thin or flat cheeks.

In Chinese medicine the cheek area is crucial in making a diagnosis. It is the colour of the cheeks which allows one to pinpoint many different changes in the state of health. The health risks signalled by red cheeks are problems with the lungs and high blood pressure. If the cheeks shine a deep red, then the heart and gallbladder are particularly at risk. If a red rash suddenly appears in the region of the cheeks, the person concerned should be aware of possible disturbances in the stomach or intestines. If the cheeks take on a bluish or a greenish tinge, this indicates unhappiness in relationships. Very dark or blackish cheeks are a sign of great unhappiness or at least a deterioration in personal circumstances. Traditional wisdom says that we should pay attention to birthmarks or moles in the cheek area. This warns that, should a mole suddenly disappear or any change take place (in particular between the ages of 40 and 42), a doctor should be consulted. In China they say: 'This is a sign of great treachery.'

At a time like this they will recommend that no arduous journeys should be undertaken and that long car journeys should also be avoided, if possible.

Round, high cheeks

Anyone who tries to cheat a person with high cheek bones had better think twice about it, according to the old masters of *Siang Mien*. There is something in this statement because cheeks like this are a sign of courage, energy, toughness and a strong will.

It is inconceivable that these strong characters would ever be satisfied with mediocrity. Sometimes their dynamism can make their fellow men a little anxious. But more frequently, at work in particular, they allow themselves to be carried away by their energy.

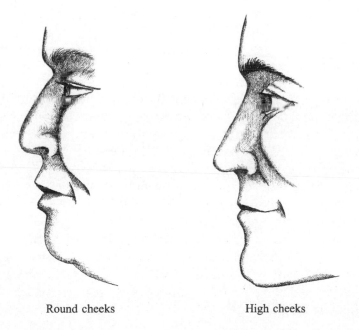

Round cheeks   High cheeks

Nothing spurs on people with round, high cheeks more than the prospect of success and career advancement. They are therefore also in constant danger of becoming overbearing and occasionally arrogant.

As a rule they reach the peak of their rapid rise at work before the age of 45. Anyone who has not managed to make a name for himself by that time, whether as an entrepreneur, a manager or perhaps even as a politician, must display other characteristics in his face which imply strong negative tendencies.

Women with round, high cheeks have the last word, not just at work, but particularly in the home. And they like to project the image of a woman who is quite capable of managing career, marriage and a family successfully.

Closer examination of the love life of those who are spoiled by success reveals certain conflicts. It is very probable that their tendency to set themselves up as the boss will make things very difficult for them in a personal relationship. Only very rarely will their partner be able, or indeed willing, to tolerate such domination for any length of time.

Bony high cheeks

If the high cheeks are not rounded, but very clearly bony, we are dealing with people who are actually clever, but who don't like to say much, least of all about themselves. Usually they are loners—and this is only partly of their own choosing. For these serious, usually good-looking, people frequently seem to be condemned to loneliness by fate. As a rule they have few friends. And these will rarely take the trouble to stand by them when they are needed.

These characters seldom have financial difficulties. But there will be phases in their lives during which they will have to cope with some serious problems. Then they may feel extremely unhappy and long for love, though they seldom manage to acknowledge this.

Bony high cheeks

Since these people are extremely attractive erotically to the other sex, they often have several relationships, one after the other and each typical of their particular time of life. But *Siang Mien* also warns that they will have to be prepared for harsh strokes of fortune or a sudden loss.

Flat cheeks

Siang Mien classifies a person who has flat cheeks as someone who prefers to avoid conflict and provocation. At worst, cheeks like this are a sign of cowardice and fickleness.

Their inherent lack of discipline will cause many fiascos in their working life. These people are rarely good colleagues, because they lack the staying power to follow work they have started through to the end and are only too willing to pass it on to others.

Though one would assume that this way of working would make them unpopular with their colleagues, this doesn't seem to be the case at all. For they are past masters of the art of employing their charm in a very purposeful way. Although they have little ambition, there are occasions when this helps them to attain an important position. For them, success is always less a question of hard work than of a dramatic stroke of luck.

As a rule these people manage their money carelessly and are thus naturally very popular with their friends. But whether they are also able to afford this generosity is another question.

Now and again women with flat cheeks seem to be rather unemotional. *Siang Mien* says that after marriage they have a tendency to sever all ties with their family home and devote themselves exclusively to their own family. Even though they are not known as fantastically expressive lovers, they do have the ability to make themselves indispensable to their partners through their enormous tolerance and understanding.

Flat cheeks

Ears

During the time between birth and fourteen years the ears give the most reliable clue to the interpretation of a person's future—so says the Chinese art of reading faces. Generations of *Siang Mien* masters have amassed a number of important findings about the ears.

It is generally agreed that the bigger the ears, the better. Large, well-formed ears—smooth and round, soft and thick—indicate intelligence and a long life.

To find out whether your ears are well positioned, you must draw an imaginary horizontal line level with the eyebrows and another below the tip of the nose. If your ears lie between these two lines you can look forward to a brilliant future. One glance in the mirror will surprise you: most of us have ears that are positioned either too high or too low.

People whose ears jut out above the line of the brows have an increased chance of being quite famous in their youth. But this is no guarantee that happiness and fame will be lasting. Ears that are situated lower down, which do not come up as far as the line of the brows, usually signal that success will not come until late in life.

According to *Siang Mien* the earlobes are linked to your degree of wisdom, but from them you should also be able to gauge a man's potency. The ideal earlobe is large and fleshy. Then you can look forward to happiness, wealth and a long life. A Chinese proverb says: 'The fatter the earlobe, the fatter the purse.' Asiatic experts will have noticed that, without exception, the earlobes on statues of the Buddha are portrayed as extremely large. Understandably, for the Buddha is the symbol of happiness and wealth personified.

If the earlobes are really thick, but pendulous, this indicates not just a long, glorious life without money worries, but also that such people are quite incredibly free with their money. Happiness has come to them far too easily—and they may perhaps find out all of a sudden that they are broke.

The Chinese associate small earlobes with meanness and enormous greed for money. As characters these people are considered boring because they have few other interests apart from money. Moreover, all the signs are that blocked feelings can lead to depression—and all too often may even spoil such people's enjoyment of sex.

The prognosis for those whose earlobes are attached to the sides of their heads is less favourable, according to *Siang Mien*. These people will themselves create the obstacles in their lives, through their enormous ambition and their unpleasant bourgeois attitudes.

Ears that lie flat to the head

Ears that lie flat to the head indicate very sensitive characters who may well possess an aptitude for extrasensory perception. Every now and then this causes problems for them, for their premonitions often make them anxious and adversely affect the decisions they make.

People with ears that lie flat to the head tend to suffer quite

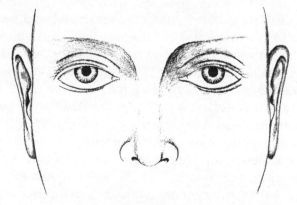

Ears that lie flat to the head

a few serious setbacks between the ages of 20 and 30, but these strengthen their character and therefore frequently mark the beginning of an extraordinary upswing in their fortunes.

These people need emotional as well as financial security in order to feel happy. If they find this, they can devote all their efforts to getting on in life. But their overcautiousness may prove to be a disadvantage if they let too many chances slip by unexploited.

People whose ears lie flat to the head have a sensual personality, can show a great deal of passion and cannot hide their feelings. But their love life will be more conventional than original, for a willingness to experiment is simply not one of their strengths.

Incidentally, in China they think that people whose ears lie so flat to their heads that you can't even slip a finger behind them will live to be very old.

Sticking-out ears

Ears that stick out usually indicate that we are dealing with a scholar and a quick thinker who is constantly searching for new knowledge. But a certain stubbornness is also characteristic of this person: anything outside his or her way of thinking will be ignored. It sometimes happens that people of this type neglect their bodies to concentrate exclusively on brainwork, and then suddenly learn to their amazement that their health has deserted them.

These personalities are also very clever—they need a great deal of recognition and cosseting. Men frequently seek refuge with strong women, who they confidently expect will protect them. They themselves know full well that they are often the weaker one in a relationship, but they won't admit it to anyone.

They know how to get on well with other people and always have a ready ear for their problems. Since they have no great

Sticking-out ears

expectations for themselves they will be very happy if their work is appreciated and they are respected for it.

Ears high on the head

Ears that are situated high on the head—that is, ears that project above the imaginary horizontal line level with the eyebrows and whose lowest point lies above the level of the tip of the nose—indicate an average middle-class existence, says *Siang Mien.*

People like this make no exaggerated claims for themselves or their social position. They are the impersonal personified, rarely wishing to stand out from the crowd. This may be because they take it for granted that they must roll up their sleeves with everybody else to earn any luxury that they may allow themselves, or because they consider any pleasure to be extremely pointless.

But that doesn't mean that people whose ears are high on the head are doomed to a boring life. Just that their opinion of what makes life worth living is different from that of their fellow men.

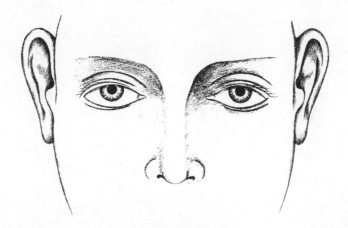

Ears high on the head

Chinese interpretation takes a different view of cases in which the ears are not just high up on the head, but where the right ear is higher than the left. According to *Siang Mien* these people have either no relationship at all with their mother or else a very disturbed one. Their parents' marriage is in danger of breaking up, usually as a result of separation, but sometimes even through the untimely death of one of them.

Ears low on the head

People with ears situated low on the head—that is, with ears whose upper edge does not come up to the line level with the brows and whose lower point lies below the level of the tip of the nose—are mostly gregarious types. Hurly-burly and action appear to be totally indispensable for these people. If they are left alone, they will in all probability feel very unhappy.

Their accommodating behaviour brings them a whole host of advantages, particularly at work. For they show thereby that they can integrate themselves well into a team.

Ears low on the head

Small ears

According to *Siang Mien* small ears point to a hard-working person who has to fend for himself or else cannot accept the help of others. Although characters like this are ambitious, there often remains a considerable discrepancy between what they want and what they can achieve.

People with small ears are thought to be self-critical perfectionists who are continually trying to prove their outstanding abilities. This type is strongly represented in journalism and the media. They love to initiate things. It fits in very well with their secret (and sometimes sinister) pleasure in tension and excitement, when everything around them is in motion.

Though outwardly cool, those with small ears can occasionally develop strong passions. But they will hardly ever rush headlong into a passionate amorous adventure. In their private life they have a much greater tendency to conservatism and the last thing they expect from their loved one is a lack of inhibition.

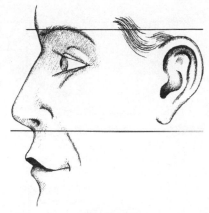

Small ears

Large ears

Siang Mien regards people with large ears as having the best prospects. To put it more precisely: large ears promise great potential in spiritual and intellectual qualities—whether the person in question has in fact made something of this talent is another matter.

Above all, both sexes have a pronounced business sense, coupled with a desire to take responsibility and give strong leadership. These qualities will have a positive effect, especially in their professional career.

Should a person with large ears show a clear interest in financial matters, the danger exists of uncontrollable meanness. And people with large ears have another weakness, if only a small one: occasionally they will not scruple to delegate unpleasant tasks and shift the responsibility from themselves to their colleagues.

Those with large ears are mostly very direct and unconventional and are accustomed to treating their fellow men with great courtesy. They owe their good manners to an excellent upbringing. They know how to engender trust, and they also

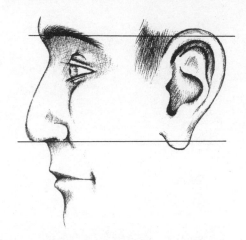

Large ears

earn it. Because of their sociable manner and positive attitude to life they are able to carry others along with them and only in exceptional cases will they spend an evening alone.

In their personal relationships these people place great emphasis on harmony. Every lover—and without one their lives would certainly not be fulfilled—is assured that he or she is the best. It should not surprise us at all that large ears are to be found on people who are known to be excellent lovers.

Pointed ears

Ears of this shape indicate a number of less fortunate characteristics. For example, these people lack feeling and sympathy. Nor are they overendowed with trustworthiness and reliability.

These people, who behave so charmingly, are accustomed to taking people for a ride. That they frequently succeed in doing so stems from the fact that others are slow to recognise the egotistical nature of those with pointed ears. One should keep people with pointed ears at arm's length, because they shamelessly trade on the good nature of others.

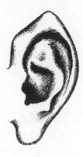

Pointed ears

But people with pointed ears are also known to be original and highly inventive and imaginative. They know how to use these talents positively, especially in a relationship with a partner. If one judges them by their almost unbelievable sensuality, in matters erotic they win hands down. Only their moodiness may deter the other sex from risking a permanent relationship with someone with pointed ears.

Other kinds of ears

In addition the following ear shapes are worthy of note:

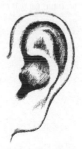

Hairy ears
Self-opinionated, eager to learn, often extravagant, rarely uses own talents.

Ear lobes attached to side of head:
Egotistical, little depth of feeling, behaves superficially, likes to go in search of adventure.

Round ears
Friendly disposition, trustworthy,
optimistic, sociable, dreamy.

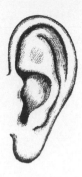

Long ears
Great intellect, lays claim to wisdom
and high morals, prefers to be distant.

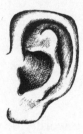

Angular ears
Shrewd, vivacious disposition,
quick intelligence, needs
constant diversion.

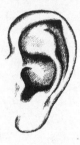

Sharp bends in the outer curves
Obstinate, stubborn, work-happy,
many-talented, must cope with great
family misfortunes.

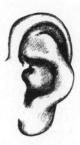

Ears broader at the top
Naïve, adaptable, easily pleased,
hedonistic.

Distinctive inner ear
A bundle of energy, creative,
unconventional, tendency to
exaggerate.

Small ear lobes
Emotional, gets involved in violent
arguments, quickly loses patience,
works unsystematically.

Big, thick ear lobes
Domineering, talented, self-assured,
goal-orientated, permanently in search
of ideals.

Chin

In the Chinese interpretation of faces, the forehead stands for heaven and the chin for the earth. The chin merits our attention because it shows us how a person's life will be in old age. In it are hidden secrets of the period between the age of 61 and death. According to a Chinese proverb: 'A nicely rounded, smooth chin takes care of the rest of your life.'

Vigour, staying power and vitality can be read in the chin— in short, the way in which we will cope with the demands of life in old age. The chin gives us general information on the state of our physical and emotional strength, how much courage we shall have to face life in old age and whether we shall manage to preserve our pleasure in life.

A good chin is one which describes a regular curve, neither too angular nor too round. It should be balanced in proportion to the rest of the face and should not dominate it.

Round chin

A round chin means we are dealing with someone who has a strong sense of family and a balanced, placid temperament. Such people exercise a favourable influence on others; when conflicts arise they are eminently suited to the role of mediator.

These people like to take on responsibility and possess an exalted work ethic which has nothing to do with being excessively ambitious. On the contrary, they seem to lack any single-minded career planning. Nevertheless, they will start to carve out a career very early on; their ability to co-operate will almost always bring them success at work.

Women with round chins are considered to be very emotional, and will happily devote themselves to the service of their family. In China they say that if a woman has a round chin, fertility is guaranteed. These women are easily satisfied

Round chin

in bed: sexual acrobatics are rarely the order of the day. Their children's happiness and a comfortable home are much more important to them; happiness in the home is frequently the pivot and focal point of their lives. The prospect of being surrounded by dozens of grandchildren will make them supremely happy.

Pointed chin

Most people with a pointed chin are extremely intelligent, but also oversensitive and tormented by mood swings. They are also said to enjoy gossip and scandal and have a tendency to deceitfulness.

For those with a pointed chin, being on their own is the worst thing that can happen. These restless characters require constant stimulation and an audience to satisfy their great need for communication.

These people also often have a seventh sense: the ability to understand the supernatural. Though whether they can trust this gift and reap the benefits of it themselves varies from person to person.

At work they stand out not just for the excellent quality of their work, but also for their ability to make quick decisions.

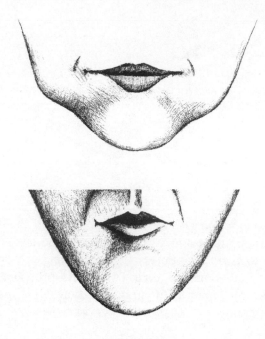

Pointed chin

Women are particularly talented in the field of public relations, whilst men with this type of chin have outstanding technical abilities.

Both women and men with this kind of chin sometimes have difficulty sorting out their feelings. This can lead to misunderstandings, especially in a relationship with a partner—for example, when someone with a pointed chin is gullible enough to read more into a flirtation than is actually there.

Men are particularly fascinated by the exotically erotic voice of a woman with a pointed chin. The trouble is that these women may be so flattered by this reaction that they rush headlong into marriage, without the slightest guarantee that it will last.

Broad chin

This powerful chin indicates an upright, honest person with a great deal of self-confidence, who may find great pleasure in work. Such people will not start anything without finishing it—someone with a broad chin appears to have almost inexhaustible reserves of energy. Success seems almost inevitable for these people, both professionally and socially.

They are well-liked for their sense of justice, though this also makes a few people jealous of them. But they have their negative qualities too: for instance, a certain stubbornness and a tendency to be aggressive. Experience shows that these character traits only show themselves in rare cases—for example, if someone thinks they are stupid. When their honour is at stake, people with a broad chin are not amused.

These people have quite a complex range of feelings—from a pronounced protective instinct inspired by a deep love for their children, to an ability to get on with others—but often they are unable to give adequate expression to their feelings for their partner. They may be afraid of losing control of themselves.

Should people with a broad chin ever be deceived by their loved one, they will leave the other in no doubt as to the consequences: they will never be able to forgive such humiliation!

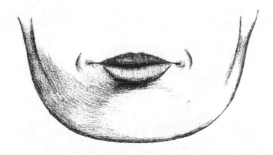

Broad chin

Square chin

At first glance a square chin indicates that the person is a fighter, energetic and vigorous, but sometimes there is also a tendency to be grim and coarse. Such characters are likely to have great difficulty coping with failure. Nor can those with a square chin cope with disrespect or injury—they can be incredibly unforgiving!

People with a chin of this shape rarely rush into anything blindly, either in private life or at work, but generally they act according to a carefully worked out plan. Life, however, is not known for always proceeding according to plan, it has many surprises in store for us. Those with a square chin take no pleasure in this in spite of all their vitality; their fondness for strict discipline makes them inflexible.

If these people misdirect their talents, energy and fighting spirit, they may fall into criminal ways. This shape of chin is often found on white-collar crooks or even violent criminals.

People with a square chin like to live the high life. If they should unexpectedly get into financial difficulties at any time, they will never under any circumstances admit responsibility for what has gone wrong but will simply write out another worthless cheque.

A love affair can easily end in chaos for these people through

Square chin

a chain of misunderstandings. Since they are not born char-
mers, they often appear to lack the affectionate repertoire
needed in love. Their rough way of expressing themselves will
be more likely to put prospective partners to flight than get
them into bed.

Women of this type are often the decisive half in a relationship—not because they like to take the dominant role, but
because they are forced to. However, experience shows that
they can be happy in this situation.

Jutting chin

This predominantly male chin shape indicates great self-
confidence, but also excessive self-importance and aggression
from time to time. Should these negative characteristics dominate, people of this type will be able to channel them in a
positive direction through sheer will-power.

These people will be successful very early on, for they
are considered to be born entrepreneurs or managers. They
have a real feeling for languages and frequently occupy
leading positions in foreign firms or in a company's overseas
branches.

However, because of their restlessness, dramatic changes

Jutting chin

could occur in both their working and their private lives. They may suddenly throw up a good job in order to devote themselves to something quite different—possibly an artistic profession of some kind. For these people have a distinctive creative talent and know how to make friends with people. They rarely need to worry about their physical well-being, for they are generally extremely healthy.

Women with a jutting chin are thought to be very career-minded—and they have strikingly beautiful breasts. They will have no difficulty picking out the right man, one who can satisfy their many needs.

But these society women also have a big problem: money. If they have enough at their disposal they can be extravagant with it. But many of them are as poor as church mice.

Long chin

Here we are dealing with a person who is emotional and often psychologically delicate. In China people with this chin shape are also referred to, rather uncharmingly, as 'horse faces'. Because of their inherent instability they sometimes have a tendency to gamble, and if they do succumb to gambling fever it often becomes an uncontrollable addiction.

Long chin

Astonishingly, those with a long chin always appear to have money at their disposal—which leads others to wonder whether they have acquired it by legal means. Certainly, with wealth goes the risk that they might be exploited by other people. But these characters also have positive traits—for instance, a talent for organisation and the ability to make friends easily.

In their work no big breakthrough can be expected. But they are not without ambition, and an important position still lies within the realm of possibility.

Luck, which is so often missing for them when gambling, is readily found in love. Men and women with this type of chin often shower their partners with a great deal of affection and are considered to be very popular with the opposite sex. Through their spectacular love life they are able to compensate for the many injustices they endure.

Receding chin

According to *Siang Mien*, people with a receding chin have very little ambition to get on in life. However, because of their placidness they are very popular. Their interests will be limited mainly to organising their life as peacefully as possible.

Receding chin

Between the ages of 35 and 50 they will achieve an acceptable standard of living, but there is a danger that in old age they will have to deal with a dramatic change in their fortunes. These people will only be able to cope with such potential problems if they learn to overcome their inherent tendency to indifference, and commit themselves wholeheartedly to their own happiness.

Cleft chin

The chin that is divided in the middle is noteworthy for its thirst for adventure and appears to be constantly hunting for new challenges. A cheerful disposition and down-to-earth character give people of this type the air of a good mate—which is basically what they are. Airs and graces and trendy behaviour are foreign to them, although they can enjoy being in the limelight.

The cleft chin is thought to be attractive, which may be one reason why these people are rarely found on their own. They will enter into many relationships and will fall in love deeply and seriously each time. They know how to enjoy the love they receive and sex with the partner they love. But no one should expect them to be faithful.

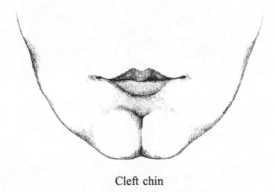

Cleft chin

Their search for perfection and perfect happiness makes them restless. But perhaps it is just this restlessness which helps them to maintain their intellectual vitality into old age. The most eventful phases in the lives of these people are considered to be their thirtieth, sixtieth, sixty-fifth and seventy-fifth years.

In work men and women with this type of chin will have it easy, but only because of their good appearance. However, they themselves must actually want to achieve something.

Siang Mien says that people like this are more seriously inclined if there is a dimple in the middle of their cleft chin. In love they have a better chance of finding a partner who is more faithful than they are, although occasional infidelities cannot be excluded. But this does not end in separation as quickly as it does with others of this chin type.

Double chin

According to *Siang Mien* there is a saying about people with a double chin: late happiness, attained after the age of 60, means double happiness. In general, a double chin is predominantly a feminine form.

Double chin

As you can easily imagine, these characters really know how to enjoy life, and good food above all. They are known to be extremely resourceful and eloquent participants in a discussion.

Their entertainment value is obvious since people enjoy their company. What is more surprising is that those with a double chin can sometimes also have a very passionate temperament.

Men with this kind of chin often have a preference for unusual occupations and a particular talent for making a lot of money. But the accumulation of wealth alone is not enough for them—they can also be very generous.

2

Moles and their Significance

According to *Siang Mien*, it is not just the shape of the face
and its individual features which deserve attention, but also
moles or birthmarks. It must be emphasised that there are
no scientific findings regarding these blemishes—which are
sometimes also seen as signs of beauty. However, the traditions
that *Siang Mien* has handed down to us on this subject are
very interesting.

Moles, which have a light reddish gleam, are usually regarded as a sign of good fortune—no matter where they occur.
On the other hand, dark spots should always be watched carefully because they are interpreted as being ominous. This is
particularly true when they suddenly change size or colour.
Then a serious change in fate may be just around the corner—
a negative change or, more rarely, a favourable one.

The forehead, eyebrows, eyes, ears, nose, mouth and chin
are regarded as being the most important places on the face
where moles are to be found and interpreted.

Moles on the forehead indicate early intellectual maturity
and a well-developed brain. If the blemishes appear right on
the hair line, then the person concerned can be pleased: they
are supposed to be a sign of prosperity. Only moles on the
temples are regarded as *even more* positive signs.

A birthmark level with the brows betrays a rather dreamy
person who sometimes even has a tendency to melancholy. It
will be difficult for such people to be really happy, in spite of
a reasonable career. If the mark is situated exactly in the

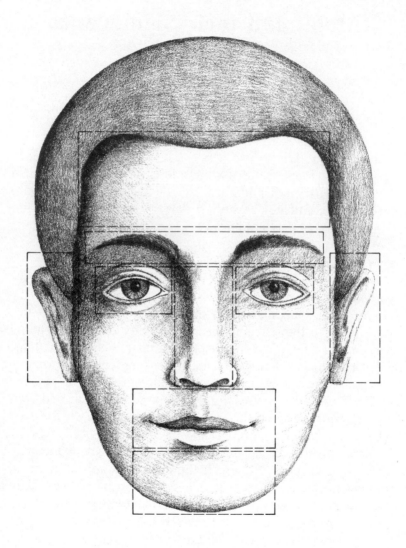

Areas where birthmarks and moles appear

middle of the eyebrows it indicates great wisdom and a pronounced feeling for the supernatural.

Moles level with or underneath the eyes are regarded as a sign of thoughtfulness. People so marked may turn in on themselves to brood and easily lose their sense of reality. Women in particular should be pleased if the spots appear above the cheek bones, for they are especially effective here as beauty spots.

Moles on the upper inner ear are a sign of above-average talent and a long life. In China moles on the nose are generally considered to bring luck. Sudden wealth may arouse envy and mar its owner's pleasure. A mole on the tip of the nose means that prosperity is constantly under threat.

A mole on the mouth indicates sensuality and strong sexual desires. It is typical of some screen goddesses to paint on an extra mark like this to give themselves an air of eroticism. But it may also bring excitement to these people's lives in other ways, not just in matters of sex.

Moles on the chin promise happiness later in life, from the age of 60. On the other hand, moles on the end of the chin are interpreted as meaning loneliness in old age. One must be prepared for rapidly increasing good luck or misfortune, should a mole suddenly appear or disappear in this region.

3

Your Fortune in Each Year
of Your Life

Having given you a broad overview of the individual facial features and their possible meanings, I would like to familiarise you with the positions of the hundred points which, according to the Chinese reading of faces, determine a person's fortune in each year of his or her life. According to *Siang Mien* we can tell from these points whether people will have good luck in a certain year or whether they will have to deal with problems and setbacks. As you can see from the two drawings, these points are in different places for men and women.

In order to make predictions about a particular year in someone's life, we need to decide whether the point in question is in harmony with the face surrounding it. You will be wondering just how meaningful each single point can be if one concentrates on that! Is it, perhaps, particularly pronounced? Is it part of the overall picture, or does it not fit in? Does a mole in this particular place indicate a painful episode in someone's life?

I would like to emphasise that, although they are known as points of fortune, these points do not in any way irrevocably determine a person's fortune. Rather they indicate certain tendencies—and experience teaches us that the chance of the predictions made about them actually coming true is quite high.

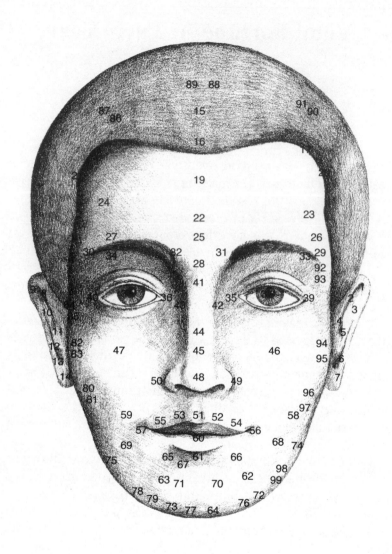

Age points on a man's face

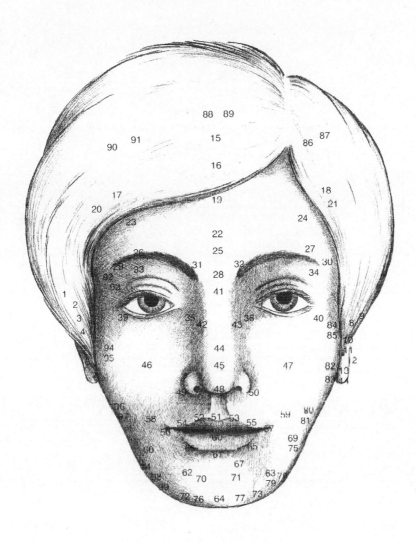

Age points on a woman's face

4

Face Reading in Medical Practice

The tradition of reading faces, though thousands of years old, still plays a major role in Far Eastern medicine today. Since a person's physical state of health is also reflected in his or her outward appearance, the face can give an indication not only of the health of someone's constitution, but also of the disturbances in its functioning and of possible disharmony. By reading faces, a Chinese doctor who is steeped in tradition can spot illnesses in his patients even before they occur. Naturally for this he needs a great deal of practice and a talent for meticulous observation.

Reading faces should not, and does not, replace other techniques of diagnosis, but it can lead to a better understanding of the context or the background of an illness. It can ensure that we pay more attention to our bodies. It is for you, dear reader, to judge just how much this is really due to the traditions of the Chinese art of reading faces. For in the final analysis everyone is responsible for their own physical and psychological well-being.

In this chapter I would like to give you some hints and tips which should help to give you better access to yourself and enable you to be rather more conscious of the signals from your body, so enabling you to treat it better.

Mouth and lips

Chinese medicine assumes that we can draw conclusions about the state of health of our digestive organs by looking at the area of the mouth and lips. At the same time the mouth and lips are also known in China as organs of pleasure; they should reveal our feelings.

According to tradition, it is said that if a mother eats considerably more protein than carbohydrate during her pregnancy, the baby will have a big mouth. Naturally no one can prove whether this assumption is true. But you may be able to check this yourself some time—on yourself or a person close to you. The state of the corners of the mouth may also reveal the condition of the pancreas. A mouth with damp or slightly wet corners may suggest the ancient Chinese opinion that it is over- or under-functioning.

The tongue is also part of the mouth area. Its colour is crucial in a medical diagnosis. The first thing that a doctor—in the West as well—asks at a consultation is, 'Show me your tongue.' A dark red tongue may be a sign of inflammation or an actual disorder in the area of the stomach and intestines. Circulatory problems are assumed to be the cause if it has a white sheen. Sometimes an exhausted digestive system is also behind it. A yellow tongue is associated with inflammation in the area of the gallbladder, giving rise to a shortage of bile. And a bluish violet-coloured tongue indicates that a person has consumed too much sugar or, possibly, has taken too much medicine.

Eyes and eyebrows

As we have seen, the eyebrows can give an indication of the function of the kidneys. In China they say that the kidney is the passive energy of the body. But the eyebrows can also show which parent has most influenced a person's inherited features. If a child is more strongly influenced by the father's side of the family, the left eyebrow will be thicker and broader than the right. On the other hand, if the mother's hereditary genes are dominant, that is indicated by a thicker and broader right eyebrow.

In China it is considered a rule that the longer the eyebrows, the longer the life. However, no one should be upset about having eyebrows that are too short. If they also grow very thick the old masters of *Siang Mien* assumed that personality to be active, healthy and very robust.

If hair grows between the eyebrows, they say it points to a susceptibility to disorders of the liver, kidneys, spleen or pancreas. These susceptibilities may be due to an excessive consumption of food of animal origin, especially milk products, or food that is too fatty.

One can glean important information on the general state of health from the colour in and around the eye area. But one must be aware that the colour can change from day to day and also reflect changes in our physical health. So dark rings around the eyes may be a sign of physical exhaustion or a feeling of exhaustion. But in Chinese medicine food with too much salt or foods which are predominantly fried or dried are possible causes which deserve consideration.

Reddish rings around the eyes can be ascribed to an overtaxed circulation, brought about by nervous strain. Sometimes a person like this also complains of cold hands and feet. In women, reddish rings around the eyes may also be due to period pains.

As I have said, all these statements originate in traditional Chinese lore. Whether they also apply to you, only you can say!

5

Sexuality and Face Reading

Flirting

Flirting is basically nothing more than a human courtship display whose one and only purpose for our forefathers was to initiate the act of procreation. Since then we have made an art form of what was originally designed with that one specific aim in mind. Flirting is both an entertainment and a conversation with a single purpose—to send signals to another person: I find you terrific, you have awakened my interest, I want to get to know you better! And: you arouse me sexually!

Our brain registers all these signals within a few seconds. As a rule we are not even aware of this. Nor are we aware that these seconds or fractions of a second will decide the success or failure of this attempt at flirting.

We notice very quickly whether the person we are with is prepared to flirt. More precisely, we read it in the other's face.

In responding to this contact we usually proceed in a rather more refined and subtle manner than our forefathers did—though there are times when we are much more direct. Anyone who has ever made a close study of human behaviour patterns will know that not only the state of mind and the mood, but also the intentions of the other person can be assessed very accurately. Exactly what else happens when we start flirting? First we have to differentiate between the flirting behaviour of men and women.

A man demonstrates a kind of hunting instinct. He tries to attract the attention of the girl he has singled out by talking loudly, laughing deliberately and making exaggerated gestures.

If he is part of a group he will quite unconsciously try to detach himself from it. From the very outset he will try to suppress any connection with the others, so that she will see him as an individual. If she should look at him, he will try to maintain eye contact for as long as possible. Then his eyes will quite automatically wander over her breasts, hips and bottom down to her legs.

It is interesting that, quite instinctively, a man's glance lingers particularly long and intensively on the parts of the female body between the waist and the hips. For this area has a special significance for sexuality and reproduction.

To some extent women behave in a similar way whilst flirting, though in certain details they act quite differently. In general they feel safer in a group, and sometimes they even need a feeling of female solidarity—especially if there is a danger that their attempt at flirting might end in failure.

If a man has aroused a woman's interest, she will cast a quick glance over him and immediately look away again. If eye contact is reciprocated, she may let her eyes linger a little longer on his face and then slowly lower her eyelids. After that she will give him a couple of quick, seemingly casual, glances. At the same time, perhaps, she will start to run her fingers through her hair and her tongue over her lips. Both indicate unmistakable sexual desire. Her laughter will not be at all loud, but seductive and low. Unconsciously her fingers will glide caressingly over her neck, and sometimes over her arms as well.

Certain masculine elements can be observed in the flirting behaviour of an emancipated woman with a successful career. She doesn't need the security of a group in order to begin flirting, but immediately tries to make direct eye contact with the man. She looks at him openly, sometimes even goes on the offensive by winking suggestively. She may let her tongue glide alluringly over her lips. Her gestures seem less than restrained, and may quite openly invite him to come closer. In her flirting game she is well aware of the risk of being rebuffed; never would her self-confidence allow her to lose her cool in the event of failure.

Siang Mien says that men and women whose right eyebrow is more prominent than the left rarely enjoy flirting. They obviously find it difficult to make a snap decision about a certain type of partner.

Men whose eyebrows are set far apart are rather shy and restrained and must make an effort to look twice at a woman. This is a great pity, for these very shy men have an extremely good chance with women, possibly because they appeal subconsciously to their maternal instinct.

Women with upward-slanting eyes love flirting. They will boldly fix their gaze on the man of their choice and signal their readiness for a little adventure by looking deep into his eyes.

Women with large eyes are most sought after by men as an object of flirtation. They need do nothing because they can be confident that a glance from their beckoning eyes will make men's hearts beat faster. Women whose nose is tilted downwards at the tip are considered to be past masters at the art of flirting.

Signals of desire

The intentions behind an episode of flirting may vary considerably: some simply promise an enjoyable, amusing conversation, whilst others flirt with the express intention of 'picking someone up'. So flirting can either be a prelude to what is known as a 'one-night stand' or the beginning of a stable relationship. Or it may just end in an exchange of telephone numbers and a beautiful memory; in this case women will simply enjoy being found attractive and desirable by a man.

If sex is the express intention of the flirtation, the atmosphere between the two people flirting will change accordingly: it will be electric and exciting, it will arouse them. Explicit suggestiveness will appear in the conversation, with the intention of testing the reactions of the other person to see how ready he or she is to respond. With luck the other will understand through these hints that matters are looking very promising.

Tender feelings, subconsciously communicated through body language, should signal to a partner exactly what is in store. The look will become more flirtatious. Playing with words sends out a number of mysterious coded messages, all of them promises of expected passion. The partner in a flirtation must be prepared to get involved in this dalliance.

Willingness to give oneself sexually to another can be inferred from many small, more or less hidden, signals. In men, for example, the voice will become noticeably deeper and huskier, whilst women will take on a softer colouring. In both sexes, breath comes more quickly, the pulse rate increases and the heart pounds noticeably louder. The eyes shine and take on a moist look. The pupils dilate; in the arousal stage they can even double in size. Sentences will be shorter, and only half-finished.

In this come-hither phase sensitivity to pain and the capacity for thought are largely suspended. If an onlooker were to try to make logical sense of the conversation of two people who were flirting, he would seek in vain. The whole point of the exercise is simply to increase desire, to turn each other on.

A typical giveaway that a woman is becoming increasingly aroused while flirting is the changing colour of her cheeks. Every so often they will blush to a soft reddish glow, then they will go pale again. The movements of her body will be altogether smoother and more fluid.

Further erotic signals are: the hands, thighs or knees of those who are flirting will accidentally touch. This is the moment when the spark finally jumps. Automatically the hip movements will become more suggestive, more deliberate. The gait will be provocative, the thighs tensed. The lips redden and swell. The nostrils flare. All these features occur in men as well as in women. They can signal to the partner: I am aroused, ready to take you and for you to take me. I am ready to have sex with you, to give you pleasure and to experience it myself.

We should make ourselves thoroughly familiar with these unmistakable signs. This can be very helpful in certain situations. It can help to save us from disappointment because we shall each be able to tell when someone's interest is only feigned and their desire faked. Then our knowledge will protect us from having our feelings hurt.

If you yourself pretend to be aroused by another person, you will find that the symptoms described above are just not there. There is no harm in flirting without emotional involvement, but in that case neither of you would show any of these signs: it would just be a little light relief *en passant*.

Siang Mien knows that men whose eye colour can be described as mixed—that is, grey-green or grey-blue—usually take a great deal of time over love-making and are very patient. A woman who gets involved with a man like this will rarely suffer the humiliation of being regarded by him merely as an object of desire. For he will not just be interested in his own orgasm, but will care about the wishes of his partner.

It is extremely important for men and women whose eye

colour is mixed to be loved deeply and sincerely. Then they can be the best lovers in the world.

People with small thin lines running under their lower eyelids are constantly ready for arousal and can develop a particularly voracious sexual appetite. This characteristic is often found in people who prefer lovers of the same sex or are bisexual.

People with these little lines under the eyes have an incredible charm which they know how to use to great effect in their amorous adventures. They rarely have problems with their sexuality during the phases when they are without a partner: to them masturbation is the most natural thing in the world.

In general they are rarely restricted by any taboos, either in love or in their sexuality. From them there is no particular time or place, no unusual practices or combinations which are 'forbidden'. They do whatever they want to do. And of course they find their pleasure in many different ways and with great imagination.

However, it is not just the eye area that betrays a great deal about whether and how someone enjoys sex. The mouth also gives the game away.

People with a long, thick upper lip will be totally dominated by the urge to satisfy the demands of their own sexuality first—and so they easily neglect the wishes of their partner. No wonder, then, that those who live with someone who has a long upper lip often feel very disenchanted with love and sex, and in many cases never realise how important it is to fulfil their own desires and erotic fantasies.

For people with a large mouth their partner's arousal is as important as their own. They are imaginative lovers who know how to give as well as take, so they usually take their time reaching a climax. Men with a large mouth are regarded as unbeatably potent lovers.

A small mouth almost always promises a quick orgasm. People whose bottom lip is thin and longer than the top lip are also among the 'quick movers'.

A very fleshy upper lip, just like symmetrical new-moon eyebrows, indicates permanently high sexual tension and a readiness to put unconventional fantasies into practice—so it makes no difference to them whether they take their pleasure in the lift or, rather more conventionally, in bed.

Full, slightly pouting lips are often found in people who, once they have overcome their initial inhibitions, prefer to enjoy love in a threesome.

People who have dark lips usually know exactly what they want—in bed or elsewhere. They will not be too shy to take the initiative. They amaze their partner with uninhibited passion, but they also know how to carry the other along enthusiastically.

Women with a crooked mouth love to talk a lot—even during the act of love. Since these women know that a man can rarely cope on his own with so much verbal acrobatics, they will not hesitate to obtain satisfaction with two or more lovers.

People with bad teeth get only a limited amount of pleasure from love play. Great pleasure and also great sexual potency are associated with bald men, men with very hairy chests and those with an M-shaped hair line who also have a large mouth.

Severe, pursed lips can indicate that a person is very difficult to satisfy. It will generally be hard for their partner to arouse in them both desire and abandon.

We should also take a quick look at the ears and nose.

It is said that women whose ears are set higher than the line of the eyes prefer the traditional missionary position during loveplay. Whilst women whose ears start below the line of the eyes prefer to be on top and like to look their partner in the eyes during sex.

Fine, thin wrinkles or lines below the base of the nose, running more or less parallel with the mouth, are frequently found in men and women who hardly ever think of anything else but—sex. It is not just their desire which is thought to be inexhaustible, but also their torrid craving, their wild urge to be loved in every way imaginable.

Erotic imagination

As we know from experience, sexuality doesn't always mean eroticism, just as eroticism doesn't necessarily have anything to do with sex. But when sexuality and eroticism are combined, one should enjoy the experience as a gift from the gods.

Whilst sexuality comes from deep within, eroticism combines the knowledge of sexuality with feeling and imagination. An experienced interpreter of faces can tell whether anyone has the capacity for erotic imagination by looking at various features in the face.

Thus large, fleshy, perhaps even bulging ear lobes are interpreted as a sign that we are dealing with someone with a vivid imagination and the capacity for rapturous transports of desire. People with ears like this are thought to be perfect lovers.

It is also said that people with a small mouth are very imaginative—and very inventive: they have absolutely no inhibitions about trying something out of the ordinary.

For people with large eyes, unusual erotic games exist mainly in the mind; they will seldom actually be fulfilled. But if someone gives these people the crucial push, they may quickly abandon their cool façade and light their partner's fire in an unexpectedly erotic and seductive manner.

A well-shaped mouth with clear outlines tells us that a person is considerate and understanding. He will presumably take plenty of time over love-making and will hold back until he is sure that the enjoyment of the erotic game completely satisfies not just him, but his partner as well.

Corners of the mouth which run inwards and turn under are frequently found on people who are strongly turned on by people of their own sex. Both men and women with a mouth like this will direct their fantasies to same-sex pleasures.

A very clearly defined top lip with a V-shaped cleft or mark in the middle is a sign of great sensitivity, erotic refinement and outwardly cultivated sexual demands. These people are considered to be highly sensitive and probably even shy. Anyone who thinks that partners like this will allow themselves to be tempted by a 'quickie' is completely wrong: in general these gentle souls have absolutely no enthusiasm for quick sex. But they can very gently and with great understanding help their partners in love to experience unbelievably erotic pleasures.

Deep-set eyes in both men and women betray their unusual appetite for constant novelty in their erotic affairs and a preference for quick, direct sex without foreplay.

A V-shaped hair line (widow's peak)—often found in men—indicates an abundance of sensuality and a taste for lengthy erotic games. In all probability we are dealing here with a lover whose erotic practices are definitely on the unusual side. People with new-moon eyebrows can also be sensual and imaginative, but above all they set great store by their own satisfaction. Should their partner prefer a quick one they will keep them going just long enough to reach their own climax.

Men and women with bulging eyes are said to have a preference for group sex, or at least sex in threesomes. And even if these erotic wishes are not always realised, the secret longing is almost always there.

People with a snub nose are considered to have dreamy natures and a preference for romantic sex with rather traditional positions. They very rarely try any erotic experiments.

Pointed ears indicate a tendency to particularly imaginative eroticism. Their seductive sexual manner leaves hardly a desire unfulfilled.

Men with a bumpy nose often give the impression that they have one, and only one, reason for starting a relationship with someone: to satisfy their sexual desires. It is doubtful whether these charming lechers will pay any attention to their partner's needs. But in a relationship with people like this one can hardly complain about a lack of sex and erotic fantasies.

The mouth is the best indicator of whether a man will be wild and inconsiderate when making love or tender and seductive. For example, it would appear that a man whose upper lip describes a continuous curve lacks any capacity for understanding. He will satisfy his own needs roughly and without wasting any time and thus will show little consideration for the happiness and sexual fulfilment of his partner.

A fleshy upper lip which is straight and broad right to the corners of the mouth is found predominantly in men who can be incredibly inventive and imaginative during sex and have a liking for combining pain and pleasure. They may perhaps enjoy being ill-treated during sex by a dominant woman. But that does not necessarily mean that we are dealing here simply with a masochist. These men are able to enjoy *both* sides of SM sex. If they have a suitable partner, they can experience pleasure by taking on the sexually dominant role as well.

Men whose upper lip is as full in the middle as the lower lip are capable of losing their self-control extremely quickly. It is therefore doubtful whether they are able to bring a woman to sexual fulfilment.

Erotic fulfilment

Having learnt which of the different features we must take into account whilst studying a person's face, in order to discover something about the most secret sexual desires and tendencies of the people around us, we can attempt to decode their erotic needs with a great deal of tact and sensitivity. We will be able, thanks to our advanced knowledge, to find out relatively quickly what satisfies them, and thus be able to abandon whatever doesn't work. But it would be extremely reprehensible to use this knowledge to wield power over anyone.

It would probably be best to make our practical knowledge and advice known to our friends cautiously and with great tact in open conversation. Under no circumstances should we abuse our knowledge to gain an advantage over strangers, superiors, colleagues or subordinates. Such an abuse would clearly contravene the honourable rules of *Siang Mien*. And we should not forget how touchy we would be if it were our own sexuality under the microscope.

We should also remain aware that we cannot be absolutely certain of our knowledge. There are exceptions in all things— and also in the interpretation of faces.

In spite of all our experience in this area there is always the possibility that we may sometimes have to deal with something totally unexpected. In spite of studying this book carefully and weighing up all the features, from time to time, while interpreting a face, we will reach a conclusion that simply cannot be right. These circumstances may occur, for example, if the person we are dealing with has undergone plastic surgery. These days, the possibilities of plastic surgery effectively altering eyes, nose, mouth and even the chin and ears are almost limitless.

In spite of all the care that we should exercise, the idea of reading a face in order to determine the sexual preferences and needs of our fellow men is naturally very appealing. We shall be able to see colleagues whom we do not respect, or our boss who has often made our life a misery, from quite a new angle—and perhaps we will treat them with new understanding.

Imagine that your bad-tempered boss has dark eyes with eyelashes that grow inwards. In this case *Siang Mien* says that he has to contend with great difficulties in his love life. Perhaps you will now understand more easily why he likes to get rid of his pent-up frustrations in the office? Perhaps your knowledge can help you to be more tolerant towards this man who is actually to be pitied, and thus improve everyone's working conditions.

But why do people with dark eyes and eyelashes that grow inwards have difficulties with their sexuality? Because they are tormented by the continual fear of being a failure in bed. They put themselves under a compulsion to succeed, which brings about exactly the opposite effect. They haven't learnt how to let go, and therein lies their problem. Continually controlling themselves makes it difficult, sometimes even impossible, for them to admit their own desires and so enjoy them. To achieve real sexual satisfaction they must learn to understand that no one can be perfect—certainly not in matters of sex—and that an understanding partner doesn't expect sex with them to be perfect either.

People whose eyes slant downwards and who have one eyebrow higher than the other tend to feel that sex is something forbidden. This may well be due to an over-strict upbringing. Presumably the strictest silence was preserved in the parental home on matters of love and sexuality. These people can therefore develop an excessive interest in sex during puberty. This craving usually disappears in marriage or a stable relationship and gives way to the need for affection, extensive cuddling and the desire to be needed. But it can never be said that passion falls short during sex.

Anyone who has naturally very small eyebrows will as a rule have little interest in sex. These people regard spiritual challenges as much more important and are quite happy and contented if they can sublimate their sex drive in this way.

People with very thick brows are continually searching for new erotic experiences. One could almost believe that they think of nothing else. Because their desires are excessive they will only rarely find fulfilment, since they run away at the slightest disappointment. Their partner in love will only rarely give them the chance to work out their sexual needs.

Eyebrows that grow together belong mostly to people for whom pain is the greatest pleasure. At the very least there is a latent desire to enjoy suffering.

Eyebrows that slope downwards suggest that these people have some difficulties with their sex life. Their greatest problem may be that they are terribly inhibited. But if they meet a dominant, active partner who is unaware of their sexual embarrassment, they can learn to take pleasure from physical love.

Women with eyes that slant downwards are considered to be shameless and sexually promiscuous. They get their greatest enjoyment in bed from being treated by their lover as a slave of pleasure.

Men with bulging eyes prefer wild, passionate sex. In the process they use their partner more or less as an object of desire and no more. This concentration on their own gratification could be the reason why they often feel very lonely and are constantly in search of new partners.

People with rectangular eyes are sometimes considerably inhibited, which gets in the way of their sexual satisfaction. They are often worried that they will lose control over their feelings and pull back before the act of love can bring them fulfilment. They will only discover the euphoria of sexual pleasure if they can break down the barriers of their inhibition.

People who have noticeably pale eyes are very quickly satisfied in love. They attach little importance to the refinements of love-play; for them sexuality is a quick fix forever in need of new peaks. Their frequent changing of partners must not be seen as an inability to be faithful; they just need the stimulus of something new in order to reach orgasm.

Men and women with dark eyes are generally reserved and love very intense, very varied sex. And they are considered to be passionate and permanent lovers. Quite a lot of effort is needed to draw them completely out of their reserve. But once they have abandoned their restraint there is no stopping them, and they bubble over with an imaginative eroticism that will take their partner's breath away.

Women with conspicuously large eyes are considered to be easily aroused and are quick to reach a climax.

6

The Facial Guide to Relationships

Many couples today do not lead happy lives, mostly because they have never learnt to see as other people see, to hear as other people hear or to feel from the heart as other people feel.

They start by assuming, wrongly, that they know what the other is thinking or feeling, but they rarely take enough time and trouble to get inside their partner's thoughts and mind. So they fail to realise that the picture they had built up of each other may not correspond to reality any more. Perhaps when they have an argument their partner no longer appears quite so radiantly self-confident as he or she once was. Or suddenly some other much-loved characteristic may be missing. Then they feel disenchanted with their partner because they are neither willing nor able to understand what has happened.

'Friendship is not just a priceless gift but also a permanent responsibility.' To which could be added: 'Exactly the same could be said about love and relationships.' Both partners should and must be prepared to work (sometimes all their lives) on their continually changing relationship, facing up to all the problems and difficulties which may arise. In short, partners must actively work at making a relationship strong and happy so that it lives and lasts.

It is very helpful to use the knowledge gained through *Siang Mien* to find out about the possibilities and limits of a particular relationship. Using the art of reading faces we can establish what types of face are particularly well suited to each other and which combinations will have problems from the start.

In the first part of this book we learned about face shapes and the character traits associated with them. These shapes can be divided into three basic types:

- round face (Moon face)
- angular face (Wood face, Jade face, Earth face, Wall face, Iron face, Metal face)
- triangular face (Mountain face, Bucket face, Fire face)

Knowledge of the character traits of our partner, combined with the evidence from our own face, can help us to assess and understand each other better. It may also help us to explain the meaning of much of our partner's behaviour towards us.

Armed with our knowledge about the forces that unite us, for example as couples, we can avoid unnecessary arguments and misunderstandings whilst building up understanding and trust. The art of reading faces can reinforce our efforts to make our relationships more meaningful and more harmonious.

In the following pages we shall combine the three basic shapes of the female face with the three basic shapes of the male face and explain the opportunities and difficulties inherent in those combinations. The shape of the female face always comes first, followed by the shape of the male face.

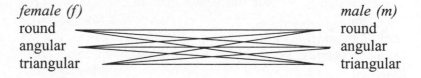

female (f)   *male (m)*
round   round
angular   angular
triangular   triangular

Round female face—round male face

As a rule, two round faces get on well together in a relationship. Both have a similar view of life and what they want to achieve from it. Both set great store by financial security and a harmonious family life.

The family also gives them the necessary strength to be able to hold their own against competition at work, to meet all the demands made of them and to stand up to all opposition. Above all, the man needs his own private oasis of calm and security if he is to be successful. Then he will moderate his claims to power and his striving for prosperity so that he never puts domestic harmony at risk.

As a rule the woman will dedicate herself to her role as the loving mother of a family, so there is little likelihood of any

Moon face

Moon face

friction arising on this particular issue. But this division of roles may be disturbed by certain factors.

As far as sexuality is concerned, both are quite conservative in their demands and will not expect earth-shattering climaxes. Reproachful scenes in the bedroom due to their partner's lack of passion will rarely occur—for neither of them will notice that the other lacks sexual enthusiasm.

A relationship between people with round faces is most likely to be lasting since they both bring with them the best qualifications for peaceful cooperation.

If two round faces meet at work, their ability to cooperate depends substantially on whether they like each other straight away. If they do, this will form the basis for good team work on which they can both build. However, if their first meeting goes badly, they will never be able to cooperate. At worst, both round faces will fight whenever they get the chance and will think nothing of plotting behind the other's back.

Round female face—angular male face

This is a very common combination. The first impression a man with an angular face makes on a round-faced woman will have a profound effect on their relationship. All will go well if this first impression signals to her: this man is strong, energetic, reliable and thoroughly pleasant.

In a relationship between these two, the woman will probably not be satisfied with just the kitchen as her domain. She will be greatly encouraged by her partner's dynamism to get a job of her own. And she will often be very successful.

A happy family life and a contented partner are absolutely indispensable for the success of her career. She must be able to rely on this support.

If a woman with a round face fails to get 100 per cent cooperation at home, her world will quickly be turned upside down. She will then have a tendency to mistrust her partner and be jealous of him, and in desperation will try to restrict his freedom.

But personal freedom and a certain amount of independence are things that a man with an angular face demands at all costs. For he feels that, as the head of the family, and therefore the one who has the final say, he has to ensure that no one in his clan lacks for anything. He sees no point in arguing about freedom with the woman he loves.

At work one frequently finds a man with an angular face in the boss's chair, or at least in a position of authority. If he has to work closely with a round-faced woman, he will be quite happy to leave the decisions to her. But if she ever calls his competence into question, cooperation will be over once and for all.

Moon face

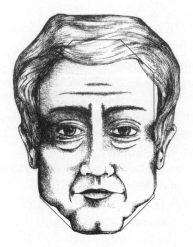

Wood face

Wall face

Round female face—triangular male face

This combination is regarded as highly explosive: a man with a triangular face can be quite unstable psychologically, whilst a woman with a round face craves leadership and security.

If these two types of face form a relationship, the woman must accept that she will be under some pressure. She will need both physical and emotional strength, stamina and a willingness to keep motivating her partner to seek new goals and so offset his tendency to self-pity. Life will certainly not be easy for her because his bad moods will cause frequent provocation and friction.

A relationship between these two also depends to a great extent on the woman's capacity for understanding the partner with a triangular face, and on the depth of feeling that she has for him. If, but only if, her extremely positive commitment to him meets with an equally positive response, the two of them will be able to get along very well together.

At work, an alliance between these two types of face will rarely be successful. For the round-faced woman there is no reason at all to defer to a business partner with a triangular face—especially since she has enough power and common sense to provide her with all the advantages she needs in her job.

Productive cooperation is quite out of the question unless she is prepared to tolerate or even gloss over his moodiness, arrogance and indecisive behaviour at work. He may possibly be able to accept her as the executive. But it is definitely better and more sensible for them to have completely separate areas of responsibility.

Moon face

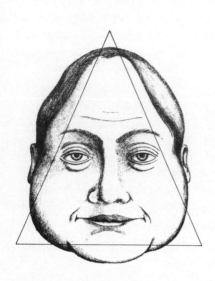

Mountain face

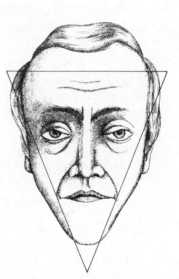

Fire face

Angular female face—round male face

This combination of facial types occurs very frequently.

As a rule, a woman with an angular face has a strong personality. She is able to make decisions, take on responsibility without hesitation, appears very self-confident and convinced of her own abilities. Once she has decided on something she will stand by that decision fully, even if the consequences are unpleasant.

A man with a round face will welcome all these characteristics if they make his life easier. For example, he will be delighted if someone will make decisions for him and look after him. He will happily tell her how much he values her care of him. If he is absolutely honest he will even tell her that he expects this of her.

Earth face

Moon face

He will be able to tell her anything without embarrassment, in a way that she will not find too demanding. If he has an argument with her—and when he does, he will get quite heated—he will do so without rancour. For he will be very careful not to hurt his partner.

Thus both partners will be happy and enjoy a successful relationship which has every chance of lasting.

Things are not quite so simple at work. Difficulties may surface, especially if the man is the boss. He may possibly resort to male chauvinism should they ever have to compete for promotion. It would be sheer agony for him if he were to be forced to admit that the woman was better than him.

In contrast to her private life, a woman with an angular face will show a great deal of egotism at work and will bring all her masculine characteristics to bear: fighting spirit, readiness to take risks, sense of responsibility, practical thinking and behaviour. She will get on much better than her round-faced opponent in this 'masculine' role.

Another factor that argues against the two of them getting on well together at work is that there will be little mutual understanding in their dealings with each other and the element of compassion will be completely absent.

The situation is more promising if the woman occupies the leading role. But both of them should aim for the same professional goals. And they should always remember that joint strategies and complementary abilities are essential for mutual success.

Angular female face—angular male face

Fundamentally there is an enormous attraction in a combination like this. For we are dealing here with a man and a woman who are mutually drawn to each other as if by magic.

Both are strong, prepared to take risks, success- and property-orientated, self-confident, forward-looking, power-hungry and independent. Both find in their partner the qualities they most admire.

So long as both of them are pursuing one and the same goal this combination is absolutely unbeatable. This is because both of them put a great deal of sexual energy into their striving for power. But once they are no longer pursuing the same interests, this combination often breaks down because they very quickly drift apart.

Both of them have an excessive amount of self-confidence at their disposal and will allow nobody, not even their partner, to encroach on their independence and their ideals. It will therefore be almost impossible for them to ask anyone for help in a crisis, even if they feel that their relationship is in grave danger. They are both aware that they can get on just as well without their partner—so why make any concessions?

Two people with angular faces working together in business can be extremely successful, so long as three absolutely vital conditions are fulfilled. Firstly, both must have completely different zones of responsibility. Secondly, both must pursue the same goal in their work. Thirdly, both must hold positions of equal rank. If these conditions are met, then they will both excel in an atmosphere of power and wealth.

On the other hand, if they don't act in concert they will inevitably clash: two strong, tough opponents who will waste no opportunity to kick the other out, or even destroy the other completely. A war of the Titans would be declared.

Earth face

Wall face

Wood face

Angular female face—triangular male face

The woman will derive much more satisfaction from this relationship than the man. She is very independent and will naturally get her own way. So she will not be particularly concerned if her triangular-faced partner finds no satisfaction in any aspect of his life and is unable to set any goals for himself.

Basically, it is of no importance to her that he feels inferior in both strength and confidence and will always be frustrated. But he for his part just cannot accept that she is the one who

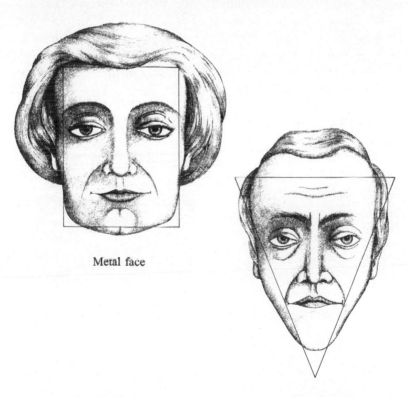

Metal face

Fire face

has all the energy, and with it the ability to realise both his, often confused, desires and her own.

This makes the man with the triangular face extremely unhappy, because he really wants to be seen as a man of action, the one who calls the tune. But he hasn't a hope as far as this kind of partner is concerned, because she will allow nothing of the kind. Her marked stubbornness nips the best of intentions in the bud.

The situation is much less disastrous if these two have to work together. Indeed, a combination of this kind holds excellent prospects of success, particularly if the woman with the angular face is in the position of authority. The man will accept this without resentment, and without feeling that his masculinity is being threatened. For in this case, he does not have to prove that he could have done the job better himself. No one expects him to be the powerful one of the team, so he is willing to accept her leadership and in most cases is an outstandingly good colleague.

Triangular female face—round male face

A man with a round face is predominantly a quiet, complacent character. He prefers to devote himself to the more pleasant aspects of life and will only rarely be plagued by fanciful cravings for power.

So he is rather helpless in the face of the dissatisfaction and continual complaints from his companion through life. At least he is clever enough never to get involved in arguments with her—his strength lies in giving in. Faced with this man's proverbially saintlike patience she eventually stops carping, because a woman with a triangular face instinctively senses that she will probably do best with this solid, rather phlegmatic companion through life. Perhaps this is the secret behind what

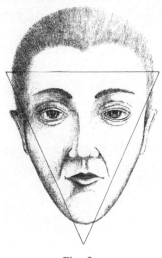

Fire face

Moon face

is often an astonishingly long-lived relationship between these two.

There are, quite justifiably, some reservations about this pair as a working combination, for neither can get along without being led and instructed by the other. As a rule the calm, friendly man finds it difficult to work steadily and single-mindedly, and in this respect he will certainly drive his colleague almost insane. In contrast to him, she really understands how to keep her nose to the grindstone (if she needs to), but usually she has no clear plan.

It makes no difference which of these two facial types is in command: only rarely will they make a successful, profitable team. There is one exception: when a third person moves into the driving seat. In this particular case, one will complement the other very well, almost ideally in fact, but only if they manage to keep their private and their working lives completely separate. He is the one who knows how to bring peace and stability to a team, while she is able to bring a dynamic approach to the work—but under the supervision of a third person, as I have said. And should their collaboration turn out less well than expected, they will at least have a common enemy in their boss.

Triangular female face—angular male face

A woman with a triangular face will be immediately drawn to the charisma of a man with an angular face. For he alone knows how to arouse in her a longing for adventure. For her part, she will have the courage to enter unknown territory because he gives her security and self-confidence. It will not occur to her to question his intelligence and authority, so that on this level she will respect him absolutely for years to come.

There will, however, be points of friction in this relationship. Because of their dissimilar temperaments they will have quite different expectations from life. On the one hand, his view is realistic and clearly orientated to the future. On the other, her

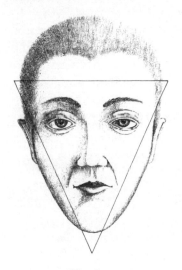

Fire face

Metal face

behaviour is usually quite spontaneous, without a thought for the consequences. The chaos she can cause through her headstrong actions leads to a total lack of understanding from her partner. Naturally she knows perfectly well that she cannot manage alone—but in an effort to boost her ego, she will repeatedly try to do so.

The foolhardy actions of the angular-faced man will provoke constant tension in their relationship. For example, he will take any risk necessary to achieve his ambitious goals. In such situations his partner's rather naïve but well-meaning disposition will curb his enthusiasm.

Serious difficulties can arise in this relationship, but only because of her jealousy. She will try everything in her efforts to curb his desire for freedom. It should be obvious that her partner is only looking for adventure. Nothing will annoy him more than curtailing his freedom.

In working life, there is nothing to prevent a long and above all successful cooperation between these two facial types. They are considered to be ideal partners, particularly if the angular face (it makes no difference whether male or female) takes over the planning.

In a spirit of comradeship, the triangular face will deal uncomplainingly with everything that the other leaves undone. If a man with an angular face has the business in hand he can rely 100 per cent on his colleague's support and confidence, even if his actions sometimes appear rather daring.

He is considered to be quite prepared to take risks, flexible and needing a great deal of freedom in decision-making. However, his partner will rarely feel restricted; the fact that he sometimes takes decisions over her head doesn't disturb her in the least. She knows that she has little chance of finding a better associate. The initiative moves from one to the other, there is a constant flow of energy through the business and a fruitful balance of power prevails.

Triangular female face—triangular male face

Here are two people cast in the same mould. It will never be a simple matter to link them together as virtually the same character—although perhaps a fascinating one. It must be realised that, in this relationship, the good aspects and also all the foibles, be they big or small, will be intensified, and that from time to time they will clash explosively.

A positive aspect of this relationship is that the man and the woman usually have the same goal in life. Hence they rarely have a difference of opinion. Both are careful to create financial reserves and to have a secure income always at their disposal. They can even be downright mean.

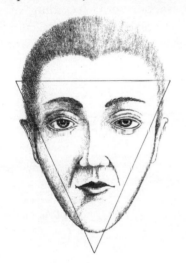

Fire face

King's face

Since both of them run side by side more or less in unison, there is a natural lack of tension in this relationship. For this reason one of them must try to tempt the other out of his or her reserve—and so be the one to supply the necessary get-up-and-go. For nobody can tolerate being permanently glued to the telly. If they both recognise their weaknesses they can enjoy quite a satisfactory and fulfilled relationship.

At work these two people make first-class colleagues, especially if they understand each other well in private. They will rarely have any difficulties together as far as job organisation is concerned. The question is, though, whether either of them is ready to take the necessary risk to bring off a big coup. Since by nature both are quite indecisive and hesitant, the moment may pass and their indecision will have cost them the deal.

But since neither of them is desperate for outstanding success and both are satisfied with a reasonable income, there will rarely be any disharmony between them whilst they work together.

7

Face Reading in Practice

How and when can I read faces?

The most fascinating thing about the human face is that each one is different. Even though amazing similarities can be detected in different people, no two will ever have exactly identical faces.

Even identical twins do not have exactly the same face. In this special case there are the tiniest of differences, perhaps in the expression of the eyes, in the facial expression, in the texture of the skin, or a hair line which does not follow exactly the same course.

How often do children hear family and friends say, 'You look exactly like your mother.' Or, 'You are the spitting image of your father.' But here 'looking exactly the same' simply means being similar.

The same can be said about character. Nobody has the same character as anybody else. They may in fact have similar features, but their behaviour and their reactions will be quite different. In China they say, 'The packaging is different, because the contents are different.' This proverb is totally accurate, simply because —as we have said—no one is really the same as anyone else.

So, how can faces be interpreted? We know that, if we understand the meaning of the individual facial features, a face can give us a great deal of rather varied information. But this knowledge alone is simply not enough to enable us to see behind the façade. We must learn to be good observers as well, and we must pay attention to details, even if they seem unimportant at first sight. And only when we understand how to combine all these elements, when we have found a way to fit together all the pieces of the puzzle, will we be able to claim that we have mastered the art of reading faces.

It is as difficult to discover the real person behind a face as it is to paint a good portrait. But you have to admit that it also has great appeal. For it promises that we shall be able to expose the tendencies and preferences that people keep disguised or hidden—perhaps without exchanging a single word with them.

Faces can be read anywhere. On the bus, in the restaurant, at the office, on holiday. We should just take care not to disturb or bother others by doing it. Nobody likes to be stared at by a complete stranger!

Whilst reading a face we should not forget that stress, tenseness of any kind and alcohol can give a false impression of a face. The result can easily be misleading.

The simplest thing to do the first time is to use your own face as a 'test object'. Decode your features with the help of this book and then, using the readings you have obtained, try to find a parallel with your character traits (which you yourself probably know best) and your behaviour. In this way you will learn, with a little practice, how to combine the interpretations of the individual parts of the face little by little into a homogeneous picture.

When you first start, don't worry if you are not sure if your observations are giving an accurate result. This happens to every new 'face reader'.

What is important for a conscientious reading is that you should always take sufficient time. Make certain you also look at your face from as many different angles as possible (this is best done in front of a mirror) before you start analysing your own, undoubtedly very interesting, personality.

So that you can check for yourself just how familiar you now are with the secrets of reading faces, some tests have been printed on the following pages. So, why not have a go?

What does this face conceal?

Five tests

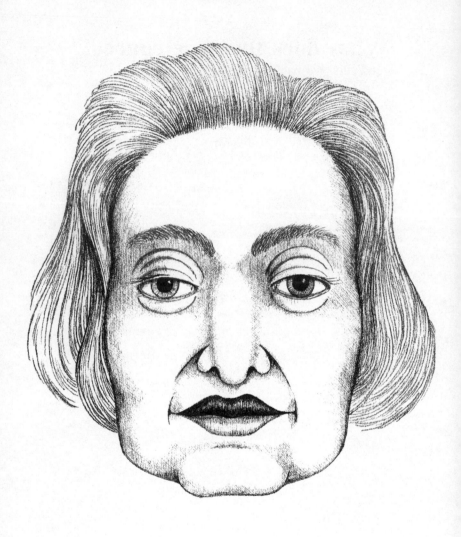

Test A

Test A

1 Does this woman's face conceal the ability to assert herself?
2 Does she have a sense of justice?
3 Does she listen to her feelings when making decisions?
4 Does she have any problems with her stomach?
5 Can this woman work independently?
6 Does she take a great deal of care in her work?
7 Does she have a robust constitution?
8 Does she have a thirst for adventure, whilst at the same time searching for security?
9 Is she easily aroused?
10 Does she like to be in the limelight?
11 Does she find it difficult to make friends?
12 Is money important for this woman?
13 Is she jealous?
14 Would she be good at teaching?
15 Does this woman seem arrogant?
16 Does she make friends easily?
17 Is this woman generous?
18 Does she behave impulsively?
19 Can she do without status symbols?

Answers to Test A: 1. Yes (Metal face); 2. Yes (Metal face); 3. No (Metal face); 4. Yes (Metal face); 5. Yes (arched hair line); 6. No (thick eyebrows); 7. Yes (thick eyebrows); 8. Yes (thick eyebrows); 9. Yes (large, round eyes); 10. Yes (large, round eyes); 11. No (large, round eyes); 12. Yes (hooked nose); 13. Yes (hooked nose); 14. Yes (hooked nose); 15. Yes (pouting lips); 16. Yes (pouting lips); 17. No (square chin); 18. No (square chin); 19. No (square chin).

Character: A woman with many positive features: a sense of justice, the ability to assert herself, practical intelligence, the ability to fit in with others (Metal face, arched hair line). From time to time she is confronted by a wave of disapproval from others close to her because she is thought to be arrogant (protruding mouth, pouting lips). She will certainly enjoy appearing before the public and giving clever performances, but she will if possible avoid moving into the foreground herself (round eyes). She can usually make up for not doing things carefully enough at work and for her dislike of attention to minor details by using her wonderful memory and quick intelligence. In her private life this cool intellectual likes to be with other people; she is sociable and loves to hurl herself into the thick of parties (round eyes, square chin). But it will not be easy for her to enter into a stable relationship because her intellect always triumphs over her feelings. In fact, others will sometimes envy her because she can throw herself into ever new affairs enthusiastically and with a thirst for adventure (square chin), but after numerous failed relationships she will slowly lose her faith in love. It may be that it is her unrequited feelings that are to blame if she complains of stomach pains from time to time.

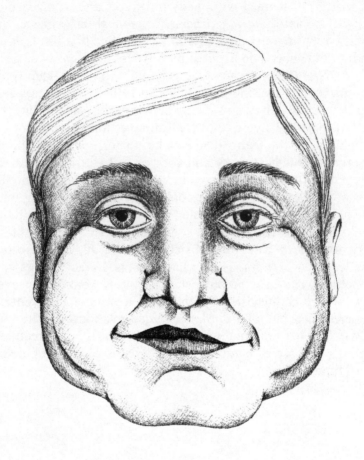

Test B

Test B

1   Does he behave like someone who takes life lightly?
2   Is he self-confident and self-controlled?
3   Can he cope with problems?
4   Is he under pressure at work?
5   Does this man have a creative talent?
6   Is he patient?
7   Is he a loner?
8   Is he romantically inclined?
9   Does this man have the airs and graces of a snob?
10   Is he trustworthy?
11   Is it important to him to be socially acceptable?
12   Can this man be discreet?
13   Does he appear to be sincere?
14   Does he have a secret predilection for three-sided relationships?
15   Does this person like to make decisions?
16   Does he have a feeling for extrasensory perception?
17   Is he sensitive?

Answers to Test B: 1. No (Wall face); 2. No (Wall face); 3. No (Wall face); 4. No (Wall face); 5. No (Wall face); 6. Yes (wide-set eyebrows); 7. No (wide-set eyebrows); 8. Yes (deep-set eyes); 9. Yes (straight nose with straight tip); 10. Yes (straight nose with straight tip); 11. Yes (straight nose); 12. No (crooked mouth); 13. No (crooked mouth); 14. Yes (crooked mouth); 15. No (ears set flat to the head); 16. Yes (ears set flat to the head); 17. Yes (ears set flat to the head).

Character: We are apparently dealing here with a person weighed down with problems, who has to cope with a mountain of difficulties. At least he thinks he does. And he is also firmly convinced that he will find no solution to these problems. The biggest obstacle, however, may be the deep-seated mistrust with which he treats everybody and everything (Wall face). He is indecisive and unsure and is totally lacking in courage. He will also sometimes be tormented by extrasensory perceptions which worry him.

There is another side to his temperament: He has a craving for social acceptance; he is very vain and from time to time he can strike people as repellent because of his boasting. But deep down inside he is also romantic and sensitive (deep-set eyes)—and he has great creative skill. He is also immensely popular with his fellow men because he shows them such patience and understanding.

In his youth he is frequently a real live-wire. One minute he is having a mild flirtation here, the next he is throwing himself into a passion somewhere else (crooked mouth). He never seems to find what he is looking for—because he often doesn't actually know what it is he is looking for.

As the years go by he will become more settled. But he will never stop searching. There is always a chance that at some stage he will set himself a clear goal and not always remain entangled in the trivialities that litter his path.

Test C

Test C

1 Can this man take criticism?
2 Is he enterprising and sociable?
3 Is he ambitious at work?
4 Can he manage to forge a really meaningful relationship?
5 Does he seem stupid or uneducated?
6 Is he a coward?
7 Is he truthful?
8 Has this man experienced many disappointments?
9 Does he appear to be trusting?
10 Docs he have any career prospects?
11 Does he have a tendency to depression?
12 Is he regarded as an individualist?
13 Is he quick to take offence?
14 Does this man need the admiration of others?
15 Is he sometimes irresponsible?
16 Can he be very passionate?
17 Is this man stubborn?
18 Does he take an interest in other people's problems?
19 Docs he like to call the shots in a relationship?
20 Does he place a lot of emphasis on his health and his outward appearance?

Answers to Test C: 1. No (Mountain face); 2. No (Mountain face); 3. Yes (Mountain face); 4. No (Mountain face); 5. No (broad forehead); 6. No (broad forehead); 7. No (broad forehead); 8. Yes (wide-set eyes); 9. Yes (wide-set eyes); 10. No (wide-set eyes); 11. Yes (eyebrows that meet); 12. No (eyebrows that meet); 13. Yes (eyebrows that meet); 14. Yes (large mouth); 15. Yes (large mouth); 16. Yes (large mouth); 17. Yes (sticking-out ears); 18. Yes (sticking-out ears); 19. No (sticking-out ears); 20. No (sticking-out ears).

Character: We are dealing here with a brilliant academic who is strong-willed and has a quick intellect (Mountain face with a broad forehead). He will be ready to go down unusual paths and accept risks if he believes in something. He has no inhibitions about criticising other people if he thinks he is in the right. Sometimes he can also be downright violent and loud-mouthed. However, he himself finds it very difficult to take criticism, and occasionally he explodes with rage.

At work he feels at his best in a team of clever people. He can fit in very well with a group and is considered an excellent listener. He is fair and honest, and from time to time his devotion to the truth is shocking.

In his private life he is regarded as a passionate lover (large, full mouth), but one who is rarely willing to enter into a permanent relationship. Sometimes a relationship with a partner fails simply because he is suspicious, for, due to his deplorably trusting nature where emotions are concerned, he usually has a string of bad experiences behind him.

Since his state of health is generally very robust, he tends to neglect himself physically (sticking-out ears).

Test D

Test D

1 Do outward appearances make this person conspicuous?
2 Is she mentally fit and bubbling over with ideas?
3 Is she always successful at work?
4 Do her relationships seem permanent?
5 Is she very trusting?
6 Is this person easily adaptable?
7 Is money very important to her?
8 Does she have staying power?
9 Is this person an optimist?
10 Does she take problems seriously?
11 Does she like to exploit others for her own ends?
12 Can she be gentle?
13 Is this person selfless?
14 Is she strong-willed?
15 Can she be trusted in business?
16 Does she prefer permanent, quiet relationships?
17 Does this person have enough stamina?
18 Is she successful at work?
19 Is she considered mean?
20 Does she lack self-confidence?
21 Is this a typical businesswoman?
22 Does she like committing herself?
23 Does she think prestige is important?
24 Is she flexible in her choice of profession?

Answers to Test D: 1. Yes (Fire face); 2. Yes (Fire face); 3. No (Fire face); 4. No (Fire face); 5. No (Fire face); 6. Yes (widow's peak); 7. Yes (widow's peak); 8. No (widow's peak); 9. No (downward-sloping eyebrows); 10. Yes (downward-sloping eyebrows); 11. Yes (downward-sloping eyebrows); 12. No (downward-sloping eyebrows); 13. No (bulging eyes); 14. Yes (bulging eyes); 15. No (bulging eyes); 16. No (bulging eyes); 17. No (small snub nose); 18. No (snub nose); 19. No (snub nose); 20. Yes (snub nose); 21. Yes (protruding lower lip); 22. No (protruding lower lip); 23. No (protruding lower lip); 24. Yes (protruding lower lip).

Character: This person will be willing to work extremely hard. It is not impossible that during her working life she will have more than one career. Perhaps this is due in part to the fact that she dislikes committing herself for too long a time. She much prefers to throw herself with zest and enthusiasm into a new job which, more often than not, she will cope with easily. But sometimes she also finds herself obliged to look around for a new job. In her efforts to further her career she doesn't always rely solely on her enormous power: if necessary she also resorts to dirty tricks (Fire face, bulging eyes). For she will always resort to these if anyone disputes her claims to leadership. All in all, this person will always fall on her feet and things will work out well for her.

In her private life this woman experiences many a disaster due to misplaced trust in her friends. But she recovers quickly, because she is easily distracted and sees no sense in getting upset over anybody or anything.

As a partner she can be very warm-hearted, attentive and generous (snub nose). But nobody should be deceived into thinking that there is a rock-hard core under her soft-hearted exterior. Her relationships with a partner are more often than not passionate and short, and she will leave as soon as her interest wanes. Not until later—sometimes *too* late—will she realise that happiness also calls for staying power.

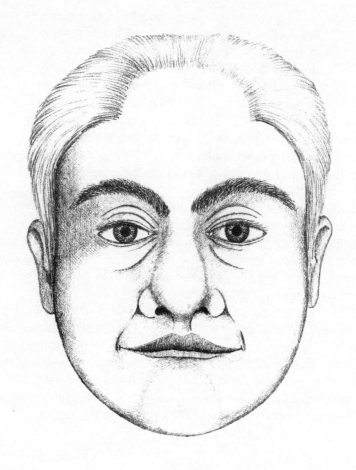

Test E

Test E

1 Does this person behave like a hedonist?
2 Is he profound?
3 Is he regarded as a typical careerist?
4 Is he family-orientated with a lot of children?
5 Is this person considered to be sensitive, emotional?
6 Where do his professional strengths lie?
7 Is he a typical loner?
8 Is this person considered to be calculating?
9 Does this person like sex?
10 What is his health like?

Answers to Test E: 1. Yes (round face); 2. No (round face); 3. No (round face); 4. Yes (round face); 5. Yes (fleshy nose); 6. The catering trade (fleshy nose); 7. No (long eyebrows); 8. No (close-set eyes); 9. Yes (upper lip thicker than lower lip); 10. Problems from the age of thirty (triple-curve hair line).